HESED

Does the Tanakh Foreshadow Jesus?

THE LOVING-KINDNESS OF G-D | VOLUME ONE

MARK STOUFFER

ISBN: 979-8-9888291-7-1 (print)

ISBN: 979-8-9888291-0-2 (print)

ISBN: 979-8-9888291-1-9 (e-book)

Note: in some cases, the verse numbers in the Tanakh are different from those in the Christian Bible. In this book, when such verses are cited, the verse numbers from the Tanakh are displayed in parentheses after the verse numbers from the Christian Bible.

Cover design and interior formatting by Rachael Ritchey

This book is dedicated to the Jewish people who have suffered so much for so long. Yet you are decent, and you try your best to follow G-d's Law.

CONTENTS

ACKNOWLEDGMENTS

Life is funny. I started out writing anonymously, and in the end, a small army of people wound up helping me. Truly, thank you all. Thank you, Amy Lyle, for doing the grammar check and limiting your corrections so as to retain my voice in the text. Thank you, beta readers, Haven Barker, Stephanie D'Amico, Collin Marshall, Behzad Namazi, Michael Tompkins, and Cheryl Walker. Your superb feedback transformed this book.

Thank you, Howard Silverman, for doing the cultural check. I appreciate you taking time out of your busy schedule to do this. Thank you, Paul Alexander, for doing the final check to thin down the repetition. Thank you Connie at Fiverr for the final proofread, and thank you Rachael Ritchey for the wonderful cover and formatting.

Thank you, Candice Coates and Audrey Frank, for taking the time to guide me through the process of writing a book. Thanks to J.R. Klein for assisting me with the pronunciation of Hebrew words and names for the audio book. Thank you Jonathan Kaplan for being willing to read the book and write a review.

Thanks to the launch team for helping me promote this book, as this is an area in which I feel inadequate. Thank you, Kamran A., Adam Anderson, Eddie Bachman, Jim Bibbo, Victoria Bonner, J.R. Cabrera, Jeff Cathis, Josh Conley, Eric Conyers, Sean Cullinan, Stephanie D'Amico, Dan Durkin, Sean Edgell, Tom Everard, Mike Fairman, Todd Friedberg, Tim Gerwin, Diane Gress, William Hallbrook, Ken Harrah, Andy Havens, Scott Herrmann, John Hoban, Jenny Johnson,

Kamran, Joe Kleinhenz, Tony Khoury, Valerie Long, Lynn McCall, Brian McLaughlin, Paul Nordman, Kay Otoa, Paul Painter, Miguel Polanco, Diane Polczynski, Dave Powers, Chris Pridemore, Dave Purvis, Patrick Schumer, Dan Scott, Jeff Seabrooks, Rich Smith, Steve Sommers, Dave Stouffer, Gilbert Stouffer, Boyd Taylor, Lisa Thomas, Al Tucker, and Oleg Vernikoff.

Thanks to my church family for your prayers.

Thanks to my lovely wife, Noushi, for all of your help and your heart of support.

Thank you, G-d. What a journey it has been with You.

PREFACE

I am a Christian. I am a layperson, and I enjoy reading the Bible. My goal in reading the Bible is to try to understand the meaning that each of the Bible authors is communicating.

A few years ago, I was preparing to write a different book for a different audience. Then one night, at 3:00 am, I awoke with many thoughts in my head. I got up and typed out an entire chapter. In that moment, and ever since, I have felt called by G-d to write this book.

I am writing this book to Jewish laypeople who want to know the truth about Jesus. I understand that most Jewish people are not interested in this subject. My experience has been that Jewish people are warm and friendly to Gentiles, but that you are not interested in Christianity, and with good reason. I have learned how you have been victimized by Christians down through the centuries. I am also aware that Jesus challenged some of the foundational tenets of Rabbinic Judaism.

Two thousand years ago, Jesus conflicted with the Jewish religious leaders, and the nation as a whole rejected Him. However, a segment of the Jewish people embraced Jesus and started the Christian movement. So too in the modern age, a small but growing number of Jews have been turning to Jesus. This book is for Jewish people who want to find out who Jesus was and what His theological positions were.

In John 5:39, in one of His debates with the religious leaders, Jesus said, "You search the Scriptures, because you think that in them you have eternal life; and it is these that bear witness of Me . . ." In this book, we will examine the Tanakh in order to see whether Jesus' claim is fictitious or real.

INTRODUCTION

Surely, the ultimate author of the Tanakh is G-d.

Christians believe that the Tanakh, or Hebrew Bible, predicted Jesus.

In this book, and in three additional volumes, we will examine five elements in the Hebrew Bible that appear to forecast Jesus. These elements are:

1. Sacrificial atonement in the Torah
2. A series of Biblical heroes who had experiences that were similar to what happened to Jesus
3. The prophecy of the Hebrew Bible
4. G-d's plan for humanity
5. The incompleteness of the Hebrew Bible, in which the issue of our moral guilt is not decisively resolved

The question is, are these lines of reasoning merely interesting, or are they more than that? Is it simply that Christians are overzealous, and they read too much into these lines of reasoning? Or could it be that G-d purposefully inserted these elements in the Hebrew Bible to enable people to identify Jesus as the Messiah?

part one

THE HEBREW BIBLE

1

THE JEWISH LAITY

The Jewish people have typically been loyal to their leaders throughout history. The problem is that not all of their leaders were worthy to be followed. Some of them, like Moses, Joshua, and David, loved G-d. But some, like Jeroboam and Ahab, did not care for Him. Of course, the Jews are the singular people of G-d, and He is their ultimate leader. He has gone to great lengths to communicate to the Jews, and He wants to bless them. How well have the Jews done in listening to G-d and following Him?

* * * * *

In the days of great suffering in Egypt, G-d sent Moses to deal with the wicked pharaoh and set the Jewish people free. The events that transpired in the conflict between G-d and Pharaoh are well known. As the conflict reached its climax, G-d prescribed the Passover to be observed at that time and every year thereafter so that the Jews would never forget what G-d did for them in their moment of need.

After issuing the directive for each family to sacrifice a one-year-old lamb and apply some of the blood around their doorframes, G-d said to Moses:

> " . . . For I will go through the land of Egypt on that night, and will strike down all the firstborn in the land of Egypt, both man and beast; and against all the gods of Egypt I will execute judgements—I am the Lord. And the blood shall be a sign for you on the houses where you live; and when I see the blood I will pass over you, and no plague will befall you to destroy *you* when I strike the land of Egypt. . . ."[1]

Why did the Jewish people need to sacrifice a lamb? Was it simply so that G-d could see the blood around their doorframes and know which houses to leave untouched? Of course not. G-d is omniscient, and He knows who His people are. In fact, during most of the prior plagues, G-d left the Jewish people unharmed as the plagues crashed down upon Egypt; and He did not need a sign to know which families to skip over.

Also, it says in verse 12 that the blood was a sign for *the Jews*. It was not a sign for G-d. But why did they need a sign? What were they supposed to learn from sacrificing lambs and applying the blood around their doorways? Returning to the first question, why did the Jewish people need to perform sacrifices to escape G-d's judgement? After all, what did they do wrong? They were the victims in this event of slavery and oppression.

---

[1] Ex. 12:12-13.

We will answer this question more in depth in Chapter 6. But for now, let's just say that G-d had the Jews sacrifice the lambs in order to teach them something about Himself, evil, justice, and themselves. G-d was personally communicating a message to every Jewish family, and indeed to every Jew, at the first Passover. At other times, G-d spoke to Moses who then spoke to the people on His behalf. But this time, He was communicating directly to every Jewish person through the rituals they were to perform.

G-d called for each Jewish family to select their sheep four days before they were to sacrifice them.[2] Lambs are innocent, cute, and endearing. That would have been four long days gazing upon the poor soul that was about to die for you. Evidently, G-d did not want this sacrifice to be simply a mechanical ritual that busy people carried out without giving it any thought. He wanted each of them to have time to think about their sins and all the people that they had hurt. He wanted them to understand that they needed a substitute. For G-d does not just judge nations; He judges individuals as well.

* * * * *

A millennium and a half after the exodus, it was Jesus' turn to take His place on the stage of history and appear before the Jewish people. It was the time of Passover again. Jesus had been preaching a message of gaining G-d's acceptance through sacrificial atonement, and He was conflicting with the Jewish religious leaders who were emphasizing following the Law. Of course, not only was it a time of spiritual discord, but it was also a time of political turmoil, as the Jews were being occupied and oppressed by the Romans. What was G-d trying to teach the Jewish people at that time?

---

[2] Ex. 12:3-6.

A few days before Passover, Jesus rode down the Mount of Olives on a donkey. As He approached the city, masses of people were present from all over Judea and points beyond. Jesus was well known, and there were people who were familiar with Him in the crowd. At that moment, a spontaneous eruption of religious fervor ensued in which the masses were "crying out" that Jesus was the Son of David, the Messiah![3]

Matthew tells us that as Jesus proceeded to enter the city, the commotion continued. Furthermore, Jesus did not try to tamp it down as He had done previously. Rather, He contributed to the uproar with both His words and His actions. Upon seeing this scene, including Jesus performing healings and children continuing to repeat that He was the Son of David, the chief priests and the scribes became indignant.[4]

Of course, everything changed by the end of the week, as Jesus was rushed through a show trial before the Sanhedrin, found guilty, and brought before the notorious Roman governor, Pontius Pilate, in order to procure a death sentence. Pilate had an advantage when Jesus and His accusers showed up at his doorstep in that he did not have a personal stake in the controversy surrounding Jesus. Thus, he could easily see the miscarriage of justice that was taking place. So, he made an attempt to rectify the situation by going around the Jewish religious leaders and bringing Jesus before the masses. However, under the prompting of the Jewish leaders, the masses wound up "shouting" for Jesus to be crucified.[5] Pilate shook his head and relented. Then the heartless Roman soldiers mocked Jesus and nailed Him to a cross, upon which

---

[3] Mt. 21:9.

[4] Mt. 21:15.

[5] Mt. 27:23 in which the Greek word (krazo) used for shouting is the same word used in Mt. 21:9 5 for crying out.

He perished six hours later.[6] Next, of all things, Jesus' body went missing despite a Roman military detail guarding the cave where He was laid to rest. Of course, His followers claimed to have found Him, alive and resurrected.

What are we to make of the masses? After all, they were just doing what they were supposed to do. They paused their lives to come to Jerusalem and celebrate Passover, and then this happened. Twice they got stirred up and made sweeping pronouncements about Jesus. But in the end, it was their second pronouncement—the pronouncement of Jesus' guilt— that sealed Jesus' fate and changed the course of history forevermore. Subsequent history has not been kind to the Jews, as an ongoing succession of Christian leaders would go on to blame the Jewish people for Jesus' death and subject them to widespread oppression and cruelty. Indeed, words cannot express the vastness of the violence and evil the Jewish people have been subjected to over the last two millennia.

Many different players, each with their own set of motives, collided with one another in the event of Jesus' trial and execution. These players included the Jewish religious leaders who despised Jesus because He assailed their beliefs and attacked their characters; Jesus' betrayer, Judas, who was in pursuit of filthy lucre; Pilate, who wanted to keep the peace in Judea and please his superiors in Rome; Jesus' followers, who believed that Jesus was the Messiah; and Jesus, whose goals were not of this world. Caught in the middle of this conflict were the masses. To them, Jesus was a preacher and a miracle worker. They were not in Jerusalem because of Jesus. They were there to celebrate Passover. Undoubtedly, their motives had to do with simply trying to survive life in the ancient world as well as paying honor to G-d at Passover. Therefore, one may ask, what did they do wrong?

---

[6] Mt. 27:45-50; Mk. 15:24-25.

The answer lies not so much in what they did as in what they did not do. Nowhere do we read that the masses took pause and prayed for G-d to show them His will regarding Jesus. Nor does it say that they read their scriptures and discussed or considered Jesus in light of them. Perhaps they should have. When it comes to something as momentous as a man's life, not to mention the spiritual direction of a nation, people should turn to G-d and seek His will. But they did not. They just did what they were told.

* * * * *

Of course, every Jew and every Gentile of every age has a responsibility before G-d. Now it is your turn, dear reader. After all these many centuries of exile and suffering in Europe, Asia, and the Middle East, some of your people have returned to part of your land. Clearly, this is the hand of G-d. Nothing in all of history compares to the return of the Jewish people to their land from an 1,878-year-long exile.[7] But G-d is not done yet. According to prophecy, one day you will live in all of the land G-d has ordained for you. And it won't be like today; you will live in peace.[8]

We live in an age of tumult that is both political and religious. The twentieth century was a century like no other. In the twentieth century, great advances in technology combined with the age-old sinful nature of man to issue forth in two unprecedented world wars. Here in the new century, prospects for the future appear tenuous and bleak. So far in this century, we have seen 9/11 and a rise in Islamic extremism, ongoing geopolitical discord, and a proliferation

---

[7] This time span is based on the formal end of Jewish rule in the land of Israel with the destruction of Jerusalem in 70 CE and the founding of the modern State of Israel in 1948.

[8] Ezek. 34:25-28.

of nuclear arms, not to mention the issue of climate change and the COVID-19 pandemic. Of course, for many years, Iranian leaders have verbalized existential threats against Israel, funded terrorist attacks, and worked to develop nuclear arms and long-range missile systems. Today, Russia has attacked Ukraine, and Vladimir Putin has verbalized the threat of nuclear war. It can be overwhelming. In fact, it is only natural to live in a state of denial and carry on our lives concerned chiefly for the wellbeing of ourselves and our loved ones.

But where is G-d right now? He is doing something. What is He doing, and what is He trying to tell us?

What is He saying to you? You should ask Him, and you should read His message to you in the Hebrew Bible. Perhaps G-d will answer your prayer and show you His will for you. For G-d is good, and His will for each person is good.

2

THE ORAL LAW

Moses made two trips up Mt. Sinai to receive the laws that are written in the Torah.[9] These are the laws that make up the Written Law. This set of laws can also be called the Mosaic Law. In addition to dictating these laws, surely G-d spoke to Moses and gave him instructions and wisdom on how to lead the Jewish people into spiritual victory. Certainly, Moses shared what G-d told him with the next generation of leaders. But do we still have an accurate copy or portrayal of G-d's statements to Moses? Of course, that is the claim made by Rabbinic Judaism: that this set of instructions has been preserved. It was transmitted orally for seventeen centuries, and then it was written down in the Mishnah early in the third

---

[9] The Torah equals the first five books of the Hebrew Bible, Genesis, Exodus, Leviticus, Numbers, and Deuteronomy.

century CE.[10] These instructions make up a law-code that is called the Oral Law or Oral Torah. The Oral Law elucidates and adds details to the Written Law. The Oral Law developed over time, but its foundation is said to be the set of instructions that G-d gave to Moses. Thus, the Oral Law holds a venerated position in Rabbinic Judaism. In the words of Rabbi Aryeh Kaplan:

> It (the Oral Torah) is even more dear to G-d than the written Torah. The Oral Torah is the means through which we devote our lives to G-d and His teachings.[11]

The Oral Law was shaped into its current form during the period of the Sages, which extended from the late first century BCE up to approximately 220 CE.[12] The Sages, as well as the rabbis who came after them, were learned men who had good character. For example, not only was Hillel a great scholar and teacher, but he was also a decent man who treated the people in his life with dignity and respect. Rabban Gamli'el haZaqen was also a great man. Though he was a renowned Sage who had a thousand talmidim, or disciples, he was humble, and he would admit when he did not know the answer to a question. Furthermore, he was a humanitarian who looked out for the interests of women and orphans.[13]

---

[10] Rabbi Aryeh Kaplan, *The Handbook for Jewish Thought*, Volume 1, (Brooklyn: Moznaim Publishing Corporation, 1979) 184-196.

[11] Rabbi Kaplan 180.

[12] Norman Solomon, ed., *The Talmud: A Selection*, trans. Norman Solomon (London, England: Penguin Classics, 2009) xxxii.

[13] Brian Tice, B.Sci., M.Sci., *Reflections on the Rabbis*, (Grand Rapids, MJR Press, 2017) 54-70.

The Talmud contains the Mishnah and the Gemara. The Gemara is comprised of rabbinic elaboration on the Mishnah. The Talmud was completed in 505 CE. The Gemara is revered as well. Albeit, the Gemara did not come directly from G-d, but rather, it is a product of the scholarly debate that took place between the rabbis.

The goal of this book is to examine the role of the Messiah in G-d's plan to rescue the Jews and bless humanity. Before I started writing, I sought to understand the Talmud and especially G-d's oral instruction to Moses about the subject of the Messiah. For, it was my assumption that I would be addressing the Oral Law in this book. However, as I studied the Talmud, I learned that it is essentially a law-code which is made up of criminal, civil, and religious laws. Although there are references to other subjects, including the Messiah, these subjects are not emphasized in the Talmud. In fact, although there are some references to the Messiah in the Gemara, there is only one in the Mishnah. It appears at the end of Tractate Sotah.[14] Furthermore, this reference to the Messiah is a

---

[14] Tractate Sotah, Chaper 9, 9:15, T-W. My version of the Talmud is the *Babylonian Talmud* (Jacob Neusner, ed., The Babylonian Talmud, trans. Jacob Neusner et.al. (U.S.A.: Hendrickson Publishers, 2009)) which only has 37 tractates. I was able to access the other 26 tractates on the internet at https://www.sefaria.org/texts/Mishnah (accessed November 10, 2022). I searched on the following words to find any references to the Messiah in the Mishnah portion of all 63 tractates: child, son, descendant, seed, house, branch, shoot, or root of the following people: Eve, Abraham, Isaac, Jacob, Judah, David, Jesse, Solomon, G-d, and Man; Messiah; anointed; and Servant. I also searched on the following words to find any references to Jesus: Jesus, Yeshua, Yehoshua, Bethlehem, Nazareth, Nazarene, crucify, crucified, crucifixion, resurrect, resurrected, resurrection; child, son, or house of either Joseph, Mary, or a carpenter. There is no mention of Jesus, and there is only the one reference to the Messiah in the Mishnah.

passing reference. The Messiah is not the subject at the end of this tractate, and it would be hard to draw any conclusions about the Messiah from this passage. Therefore, either G-d did not discuss the Messiah with Moses very much, or if He did, the content of those conversations has been lost.

On the other hand, the subject of the role of the Messiah in G-d's plan is an emphasis in the Hebrew Bible. In fact, there is a constant thread running through the Torah, Psalms, and Prophets in which the Messiah's arrival and mission are predicted. The prophecies are replete with specific details.

Therefore, in this book we will set the Talmud aside and focus on the Hebrew Bible.

3

LITERARY DEVICES

There are many literary devices that are available for authors to use in their writing. An incomplete list would include alliteration, comparison, contrast, flashback, foreshadowing, irony, metaphor, satire, symbolism, and theme. These devices can be very powerful. Indeed, they are utilized by the greatest literary masters, from William Shakespeare to Stephen King.

Literary devices serve multiple purposes. First of all, they can make the writing more interesting, poignant, or even fun. After all, prose devoid of any literary devices can be boring or bland and make no impact on the reader. Second, literary devices can help the reader to understand a difficult concept. Third, writing that utilizes these devices well can cause the reader to make an emotional connection with the subject matter. The effect of this connection can simply be for the reader's enjoyment (in the case of fiction), or it can be to win the reader over to an argument the author is trying to make.

In some cases, a piece of literature can even inspire the reader to act or to make a change in their life.

Of course, literary devices are techniques that are available to the writer of fiction to a far greater degree than to the writer of nonfiction.

Or are they?

In the classic novella, *Animal Farm*, written by George Orwell in 1945, the entire work is dominated by literary devices. It is both an allegory and a fable, and it employs biting satire and tragic irony. However, *Animal Farm* is nonfiction. It is an account of the Bolshevik Revolution in 1917, followed by the beginning of the Stalinist era in the Soviet Union. The point of the story is that despite the grand intentions of the downtrodden Russian masses and their leaders at the beginning of the struggle to overthrow their oppressors and achieve a state of utopian equality, in the end, the people were just in a different room in hell. In a cruel twist of fate, Stalin and his fellow communist party leaders became corrupt, and they treated the people every bit as oppressively as the Czars did. Indeed, they even introduced new methodologies to control the masses, including undermining the family structure and utilizing propaganda and coercion to control people.[15]

Orwell himself was a socialist, but he had the integrity to fully expose this failed attempt to relieve human suffering and bondage. The literary devices he uses serve to make his point in a much more powerful way than a mere retelling of the names, dates, casualty counts, and outcomes of this historic event. In the story, Czar Nicholas II is represented by the farmer, Mr. Jones; the communist party leaders are represented by the pigs on the farm; and Stalin is the pig named Napoleon. Over time, the pigs become just like the

---

[15] Orwell covers these tactics in his classic work, *1984*.

human farmer they overthrew in their neglect and ill-treatment of their fellow farm animals. The irony is spectacular.

Orwell pulls no punches in *Animal Farm*. For example, rule number five of the original list of seven commandments for the newly liberated farm animals states that "No animal shall drink alcohol."[16] However, later in the story, when the pigs get into some of Farmer Jones's alcohol, we read:

> It was a few days later than this that the pigs came upon a case of whisky in the cellars of the farmhouse. It had been overlooked at the time when the house was first occupied. That night there came from the farmhouse the sound of loud singing, in which, to everyone's surprise, the strains of "Beasts of England" were mixed up. At about half-past nine Napoleon, wearing an old bowler hat of Mr. Jones's, was distinctly seen to emerge from the back door, gallop rapidly round the yard, and disappear indoors again. But in the morning a deep silence hung over the farmhouse. Not a pig appeared to be stirring. It was nearly nine o'clock when Squealer made his appearance, walking slowly and dejectedly, his eyes dull, his tail hanging limply behind him, and with every appearance of being seriously ill. He called the animals together and told them that he had a terrible piece of news to impart. Comrade Napoleon was dying!

---

[16] George Orwell, *Animal Farm* and *1984* (New York, NY: Houghton Mifflin Harcourt Company, 2003) 16.

> A cry of lamentation went up. Straw was laid down outside the doors of the farmhouse, and the animals walked on tiptoe. . .
>
> By the evening, however, Napoleon appeared to be somewhat better, and the following morning Squealer was able to tell them that he was well on the way to recovery. By the evening of that day Napoleon was back at work, and on the next day it was learned that he had instructed Whymper to purchase in Willingdon some booklets on brewing and distilling. A week later Napoleon gave orders that the small paddock beyond the orchard, which it had previously been intended to set aside as a grazing-ground for animals who were past work, was to be ploughed up. It was given out that the pasture was exhausted and needed reseeding; but it soon became known that Napoleon intended to sow it with barley.[17]

I wonder if Orwell was smiling as he was typing this passage? He appears to have been a pretty intense individual, but the satire in these sentences is so delicious that he had to be enjoying himself. Yet, Orwell did not use these literary devices to put his own slant on the communist takeover of Russia. He could have twisted the facts to suit his agenda, as do the writers of political propaganda. Rather, his purpose in using literary devices was to expose the truth more clearly, including the meaning of this historic event, as well as the motives of the men who shaped history at this point in time.

------

[17] Orwell 64-65.

The writing in the Bible is also superb. It, too, employs literary devices to communicate more clearly and powerfully the truth about G-d and the condition of man. The Bible contains poetry, theology, history, and prophecy. There are also psalms or songs, proverbs, parables, and even a love poem. In all of these various forms of writing, the Bible employs a number of literary devices. Some of the literary devices in the Bible include anthropomorphism, contrast, foreshadowing, imagery, metaphor, poetic justice, symbolism, and theme. Here are a couple examples:

1. A good example of contrast is the side-by-side depiction of the characters of the first two kings of Israel, Saul and David. Saul was a typical human king, whereas David was a king who bowed before G-d. In 1 Samuel 10, the prophet Samuel anointed Saul with oil. Then the Spirit of the L-rd came upon Saul, and he prophesied.[18] Nonetheless, Saul was insecure, and when it was time for him to be introduced to the nation, he hid amongst the baggage.[19] Later, in a precarious moment in which the Jews were vastly outnumbered by the Philistine army, Saul foolishly took it upon himself to perform the burnt offering when Samuel did not show up on time. The one thing you could not do was usurp a priestly role. This mistake cost him dearly, as no son of his would ever sit on the throne. Thus, Saul was very human. He was scared, and he had little faith and perhaps little understanding of the Hebrew Bible. Once Samuel showed up, he spoke to Saul and said:

   "But now your kingdom shall not endure.
   The L-rd has sought out for Himself a

---

[18] 1 Sam. 10:6.
[19] 1 Sam. 10:22.

man after His own heart, and the L-rd
has appointed him as ruler over His
people, because you have not kept what
the L-rd commanded you."[20]

Needless to say, Saul was very upset by these words
from Samuel. Rather than repenting of his mistake and
turning to G-d for mercy, Saul fought against this
pronouncement and tried to hold on to that which was
G-d's to give or take away as He saw fit. The result was
conflict and a lack of peace for Saul for the rest of his life.

David was a youth when Samuel went to visit Jesse
to anoint one of his sons to be the next king. When
Samuel arrived, Jesse brought out his oldest son, Eliab,
but the L-rd said to Samuel: "Do not look at his
appearance or at the height of his stature, because I have
rejected him; for G-d sees not as man sees, for man looks
at the outward appearance, but the L-rd looks at the
heart."[21] Saul, too, had been tall;[22] but that does not
matter to G-d. Next, Jesse brought out six more brothers,
one at a time. But each time, G-d indicated to Samuel
that the new candidate was not the one. So Samuel asked
Jesse, "Are there any more?" Jesse replied, "There
remains yet the youngest, and behold, he is tending the
sheep."[23] So they sent for David, and when he came, the
L-rd said "Arise, anoint him; for this is he."[24] Then
Samuel anointed him, and the Spirit of the L-rd came
upon David and departed from Saul.

---

[20] 1 Sam. 13:14.

[21] 1 Sam. 16:7.

[22] 1 Sam. 9:2; 10:23.

[23] 1 Sam. 16:11.

[24] 1 Sam. 16:13.

Still a youth, David was sent to the front lines to bring food to his brothers. When he got there, the army was heading out in battle formation and shouting their war cry. It was quite a scene. David's immediate response was to leave the baggage and run to the battle site.[25] For David was not insecure. As David found his brothers and was speaking to them, they were interrupted by the Philistine Goliath, himself an exceedingly tall man, who was yelling at the Jews and taunting them. David was incensed. He said, "Who is this uncircumcised Philistine, that he should taunt the armies of the living G-d?"[26] Of course, the rest of this story is very well known. The point is that David cared about the will of G-d for the nation of Israel, whereas Saul cared about himself. Clearly, the author of 1 Samuel was inserting a contrast into his writing to point out that the heart of a man for G-d is the quality that G-d looks for in selecting a king for the Jewish people. Undoubtedly, the writer also wanted his readers to contemplate the importance of this quality for their own lives, too.

2. An example of vivid imagery is Proverbs 26:11: "Like a dog that returns to its vomit, so is a fool who repeats his foolishness." Admittedly, the image this sentence evokes is not pleasant. However, the wisdom in this sentence is arresting. This proverb gets our attention, and it speaks to us of how it is a mistake to live our lives disregarding G-d and His ways.

The writing in the Hebrew Bible is excellent. However, the Bible is not always as much fun to read as *Animal Farm*, because in the Bible, we are not always reading about a

---

[25] 1 Sam. 17:20-22.
[26] 1 Sam. 17:26.

villainous tyrant in whom we can all take glee in being exposed. Rather, the guilty one in the Bible is thee, and it is me. Thank G-d that the Bible ends differently than *Animal Farm*, which ends on a note of hopelessness as the communists wound up being every bit as oppressive as the king they overthrew. On the other hand, the Bible ends in hope. G-d is not like a human czar, communist party leader, crooked politician, or capitalist factory owner. He does not take and oppress. G-d gives and liberates. He does not utilize violence to maintain His subjects in a state of subservience. G-d subjects Himself to violence that we might go free. In the final two chapters of Revelation, man is finally restored to the lofty position he enjoyed in the first two chapters of Genesis. He is in G-d's presence, forgiven and accepted, and enjoying a relationship with G-d.

Of course, a solution had to be provided for the problem of our guilt in order for this to be possible. Thanks be to Jesus, our savior, who stepped in harm's way and took the punishment for our guilt onto His big, broad shoulders.

*   *   *   *   *

In the next chapter of this book, we will take a look at three prominent literary devices in the Hebrew Bible: symbols, types, and patterns. These devices are used in multiple books in the Hebrew Bible. They also carry over into the Christian New Testament. It is important to understand them to be able to hear G-d's overall message in the Hebrew Bible.

Indeed, it is important to recognize whenever any literary device is present in a piece of writing. For example, sarcasm. If you miss it, then you will completely miss the author's meaning. But it is also important for readers not to abuse literary devices. For example, a biased reader could read too much into a symbol, or a reader could impose a connection between characters or story elements that is not actually there. The plain meaning of the text should be taken as the intended meaning, unless it is clear that the author is using a literary device. One must always be careful not to approach the Hebrew Bible, or any piece of writing, with a preconceived agenda. Otherwise, it is almost certain that you will hear what you want to hear, but not what the author is saying.

In this book, we will be examining many passages from the Bible. We will treat these passages the same as any other piece of writing. We will look for literary devices and try to discern the author's writing strategy. We will look up the definitions of key Hebrew and Greek words to make sure our English translation has not understated the strength or richness of the author's argument. Of course, we will also keep in mind the context of each individual Bible book, as well as the overall context of either the Hebrew Bible or the Christian New Testament. In addition, we will consider the views of Jewish and Christian theologians on the passages we examine.

But there is still one more thing. The Bible is different from other books in that its ultimate author is G-d. These are His words to us. If you have an open mind and you pray to Him for understanding, He will show you His message and you will know in your soul that He spoke to you.

4

SYMBOLS, TYPES, AND PATTERNS

The Hebrew Bible is a collection of thirty-nine different books, which were written by multiple authors over a period of approximately one thousand years. The Christian New Testament consists of twenty-seven books written over a span of about fifty years that ended approximately 1,550 years after Moses wrote the Torah. In all, there were around forty authors who wrote the Hebrew Bible and the Christian New Testament. The authors grew up in different historical settings and came from a wide variety of personal backgrounds. They wrote in three different languages: Hebrew, Aramaic, and Greek. Yet, there was one G-d behind all the authors, inspiring each of their writings.

That is a pretty big claim. If that is true, then you would expect that in some way, there would be a strong unity to the Bible despite its being written by so many different authors over such a long period of time. After all, 1,550 years would not be a very long time for an infinite G-d. In fact, G-d stands outside of time; He can see the future. Sure enough, we can see a unity amongst passages from different eras as G-d's view of man's sin remains the same, no matter which empire has ascended to the top or how much society has progressed. Hence, we see symbols, types, and patterns being employed throughout the Bible. These literary devices tie the different books of the Bible together. They also make the Bible more fun to read, which makes it easier for us to hear G-d's voice and learn from Him.

There is rich symbology in the Hebrew Bible. For example, in the books of Exodus and Leviticus, G-d prescribes in meticulous detail the design for the Tabernacle, its furniture, and all the related ceremonies and rituals. These design and ceremonial elements are replete with symbolic meaning, which we will examine in chapters 7, 8, and 9 of this book.

Another example of symbols comes from the book of Daniel. In this unparalleled set of prophecies, G-d gives Daniel visions into the future and predicts the coming of three world empires. At the time he received the visions, Daniel was living in exile in the city of Babylon during the period of the Babylonian Empire. G-d revealed to him in the visions that there would be three additional world empires that would supplant one another, and that would have a large impact on the Jewish people. Those empires were the Medo-Persian Empire, the Greek Empire, and the Roman Empire. In Daniel chapter 2, G-d gave Daniel a vision of all four empires as seen from man's point of view. The symbol that was used was a statue of a man. The different empires were represented by different parts of the body. The statue was made out of precious metals, and it was glorious. After all, this is how we view ourselves. We see our own greatness. We see ourselves as rising above the rest, and we feel we are worthy to be memorialized by a larger-than-life statue. On the other hand, G-d sees our lives and our empires differently. In Daniel chapters 7 and 8, Daniel received two additional visions of the same empires, only this time, the visions were based on G-d's perspective. The symbols in these two visions were a series of wild animals. This is how G-d sees our empires—not as glorious, but as savage and inhumane. For example, He portrays the Greek Empire as an enraged goat:

> While I was observing, behold a male goat was coming from the west over the surface of the whole earth without touching the ground; and the goat *had* a conspicuous horn between his eyes. And he came up to the ram that had the two horns, which I had seen standing in front of the canal, and rushed at him in his mighty wrath. And I saw him come beside the ram, and he was enraged at him; and he struck the ram and shattered his two horns, and the ram had no strength to withstand him. So he hurled him to the ground and trampled on him, and there was none to rescue the ram from his power. Then the male goat magnified *himself* exceedingly. But as soon as he was mighty, the large horn was broken; and in its place there came up four conspicuous *horns* toward the four winds of heaven.[27]

Here the power-lust, the brutality, and the arrogance of the Greek Empire are on display. From G-d's viewpoint, their

---

[27] Dan. 8:5-8.

crushing victory over the Medo-Persian Empire did not define their greatness, but rather their shame.

Of course, things really haven't changed much from the ancient world to today. During World War II, Hitler's nickname for himself was the 'Wolf'. Hitler saw himself as a predator, and in his mind, that made him great. Even today, we have not learned. It is not uncommon to see ranks of goosestepping soldiers saluting as they parade past dictators. In these parades, they pull missiles on carts past the dictators as if these instruments of mass-death were things to be proud of. These leaders are displaying their self-perceived greatness, their might, and their willingness to take life.

G-d also gave specific details with each of the beasts in Daniel 7 and 8 that would turn out to define each of the empires once their days came and they took their place on the stage of history. In the case of the goat, he flew across the ground at great speed just as the Greeks would go on to conquer the Medo-Persian Empire in a very short amount of time. The goat was enraged at the ram because the Medes and Persians had unsuccessfully tried to attack Greece earlier. The large horn that became broken was Alexander the Great, who died early at the age of thirty-two. He was replaced not by an heir, but rather by four generals who are represented by the four horns. They each ruled over a different part of what became a divided and disunified empire.[28]

Many such details were given in these visions, clearly identifying the empires when they arose. In fact, the accuracy of these prophecies is hard to deny. However, that is no problem for the G-d deniers of our day, who merely claim that these prophecies are forgeries. They say that the Daniel who

---

[28] John F. Walvoord and Roy B. Zuck, eds., *The Bible Knowledge Commentary*, Old Testament Edition (Wheaton Il.: Victor Books, 1985) 1350, 1358.

lived in exile in Babylon did not write them, but rather someone wrote them after the fact and claimed that they were written by Daniel.

Of course, G-d is not threatened by these self-proclaimed intellectual elites. He is one step ahead of them. He has orchestrated the archaeological discoveries of building inscriptions, coins, commercial documents, and even copies of Bible books that have largely remained intact due to the arid climate of Israel and the surrounding lands. These finds have validated the authenticity of Daniel and the other prophets. For not only did the prophets write about the future, but they also included some historical details from their times. Some of these details became lost over time. Therefore, the forgeries that were alleged to take place hundreds of years later could not have taken place, because the forgers would not have known this information. Indeed, G-d has not only provided us with a trove of specific prophecies; He has also provided us with hard evidence to authenticate the dates they were written.[29]

One of the things we see with symbology is that it gets repeated in the Bible. Each appearance of a symbol reveals something new about its meaning. The repetition of a symbol can also give an indication of how important the referent of the symbol is to G-d. Additionally, biblical symbols are oftentimes used to foreshadow a future event or person that will play an important role in G-d's plan for mankind.

Types are related to symbols. Types are real people whose lives in some way foreshadow the actions, experiences, or role of another person who has been prophesied to one day come and play a part in G-d's plan. Hence, when the future person comes along and takes their place on the stage of history, we

---

[29] Gleason L. Archer, Jr., *A Survey of Old Testament Introduction* (Chicago: Moody Press, 1964, 1974) 391.

can identify them as we observe the connection(s) between their life and the earlier person's life. Multiple examples of types will be given in chapters 10 through 15 of this book.

Patterns are similar to types, only they are not people; they are events. More specifically, they are historical events that repeat and are recorded by the Hebrew Bible every time they happen. These events can be certain kinds of interactions between people, or they can be interactions between people and G-d. Of course, G-d intentionally had each recurrence recorded in order to build a pattern to both get our attention and teach us something that is important. It is really quite ingenious. Like symbols and types, these patterns may be foreshadowing similar future events that will one day be important building blocks in G-d's unfolding plan for mankind.

A few interesting Biblical patterns include: 1. single men meeting their spouses for the first time at water wells; 2. G-d intervening on behalf of barren women; 3. G-d selecting only one brother out of either two or more to play an important role in His plan for mankind; and 4. people responding to G-d calling them with the words "Here I am."

In the case of men meeting their wives at wells, we see this with Abraham's servant meeting Rebekah at a well and bringing her back for Isaac;[30] Jacob meeting his beloved Rachel at a well;[31] and Moses meeting the seven daughters of Reuel at a well and defending them. When the eligible young ladies took Moses home to meet their father, he gave the eldest, Zipporah, to Moses to be his wife.[32] All three stories consist of positive encounters with a hint of romance in the air. In the passages, it comes out that Rebekah and Rachel

---

[30] Gen. 24:18.
[31] Gen. 29:10-11.
[32] Ex. 2:16-22.

were beautiful. In addition, we can see the inner beauty of Rebekah by the way she treated Abraham's servant. Surely, G-d has made women beautiful and attractive to men. Perhaps the lesson G-d has for us by making a pattern out of these three stories is that He values marriage and we should too. Love and marriage are precious gifts from G-d. We should be thankful for our spouses, honor them, and always remember how precious they were to us on the day we married them. In addition, as you read through these passages, another common element appears to be the wisdom of falling for someone who comes from a good family and has good character.

If the Christian New Testament is a second volume completing a two-volume set along with the Hebrew Bible, then you would expect these patterns to carry forward into volume two. Sure enough, in the case of men meeting their wives at a well, the pattern does carry forward, albeit with a twist. In John chapter 4, Jesus meets a Samaritan woman at a well. The twist is that there is no romance in this interaction. Nonetheless, there is a deep love expressed by Jesus and received by the woman. She was the kind of woman He was looking for, but not because she was beautiful. She had lived an unworthy life, was lost, and was ready to be found by G-d.[33] She may well have been attractive, but she was not chaste. She had not respected or honored G-d's precious gift of marriage. In fact, she had been married five times before, and she was living with a man out of wedlock at the time she met Jesus.

Unlike Rebekah, who was gathering water at the customary time in the cool of the early evening, the Samaritan woman was ostracized by her community and came to the well in the heat of the day when she would not have to encounter any of the other ladies and see the scorn on their faces. Also,

---

[33] Mk. 2:14-17.

unlike Rebekah, she did not kindly oblige the weary traveler and draw water to refresh Jesus. Of course, when Jesus initiated conversation with her, he crossed two social barriers: she was the opposite sex, and she was a hated Samaritan. At first she was taken aback by Jesus' forwardness. But as the conversation progressed, her countenance changed as she became aware that He was a man of G-d, and in fact, He was more than that.

She had been rejected by her own people. This had come to define her, and her actions emanated from this self-perception. It appears she even believed that G-d had rejected her. But Jesus was able to correct that misperception. He extended an offer of grace and acceptance to her, and she jumped at it. She received salvation and experienced a profound healing in her soul in that moment. Then her demeanor changed even more. She was positively gleeful. Her immediate response was to cast aside the age-old social barriers that ruled life in the ancient world. She marched into town and told everyone about Jesus. She was convincing. They followed her to the well where they met Jesus, too.

The pattern of G-d interacting with barren women is also important, and it bears mentioning as well. The subject of birth in general is an important theme in the Bible, going all the way back to Eve in Genesis chapter 3. Indeed, to bear children and to play the role of a mother is important work and a high honor that G-d has bestowed on women. Yet, some women cannot have babies.

In Genesis chapter 11, we are introduced to Abram (Abraham). G-d wanted to use him to start a new people who would be His people and His representatives on earth. The problem was that his wife Sarai (Sarah) was elderly and had been barren her whole life. In order to overcome this obstacle, G-d did a miracle and opened her womb.

Like her mother-in-law, Sarah, Rebekah was barren too. But Isaac prayed on her behalf and G-d enabled her to bear children.[34]

Like her mother-in-law, Rebekah, Rachel could not conceive until G-d helped her.[35]

Later in Jewish history, Hannah cried out to G-d in her despair, and He gave her a son she named Samuel.[36]

There is a very definite pattern here that portends a future miraculous conception. Sure enough, we find Elizabeth in the Christian New Testament. She was also advanced in years and barren.[37] In addition, like Isaac, her husband was praying for her. In fact, Zacharias was a priest, and he had been chosen by lot to enter the Holy Place and offer the incense. As he was performing this ritual, an angel appeared to him and gave him the good news. Further, the angel told him that his son would be a great man of G-d who would turn many sons of Israel back to the L-rd.[38] The angel told Zacharias that he and his wife were to name their child John, and that John would play a role that had been prophesied centuries ago in the Hebrew Bible.[39] John's role was to prepare the Jewish people for the coming of the L-rd.[40]

Sure enough, John would go on to call the Jewish people to be baptized, or in other words to be immersed into a whole new way of approaching G-d. Namely, they were no longer to approach G-d based on the works of the Law, but rather based on G-d's forgiveness for their sins. John fulfilled his role by getting the attention of the nation, announcing Jesus' coming,

---

[34] Gen. 25:21.

[35] Gen. 30:1-24.

[36] 1 Sam. 1:9-20.

[37] Lk. 1:7.

[38] Lk. 1:16.

[39] Isa. 40:3-5; Mal. 3:1; 4:5-6 (3:23-24).

[40] Isa. 40:3-5; Mt. 3:1-3; Mk. 1:2-8; Lk. 1:17.

and preparing people for Jesus' message. Of course, John was also Jesus' forerunner in the womb as his miraculous birth preceded Jesus'. Indeed, Elizabeth was a relative of Mary's,[41] and John and Jesus were cousins.

Mary's miraculous pregnancy was also foreshadowed by the line of women whom G-d supernaturally enabled to conceive, starting with Sarah. These women were promised children who would play important roles in G-d's plan, but each of these ladies was barren. Therefore, G-d intervened and overrode the laws of nature so they could conceive with their husbands and have the children they were promised.

Mary's case was different. She was not barren or old. Nor was she married. She was very young and engaged, and, as was the custom in her day, she was a virgin. Therefore, G-d had to do a unique miracle in her case in order for her to become pregnant and yet still remain a virgin. Indeed, Jesus could not be conceived the normal way because He already existed. Hence, He had to be implanted in Mary's womb. Of course, the Christian New Testament does not explain the mechanics of how G-d did that.[42] That is OK, for it was a miracle. The Bible does not explain how G-d performs miracles. For example, the Hebrew Bible does not explain the specific details of how G-d removed a rib from Adam and fashioned it into Eve.

G-d's message in the Bible does not include how He does miracles, because we do not need to understand that. But we

---

[41] Lk. 1:36.

[42] It should be noted that any attempts to tie Jesus' conception to ancient myths in which Zeus or any other god had sexual relations with a mortal woman should be rejected out of hand. Such attacks are insulting in the extreme. This is not the way G-d performs miracles. G-d did not use a hammer and nails, a saw, and a drill when He made heaven and earth. Neither did He approach Mary in the form of a man when Jesus was formed in her womb (Mt. 1:20).

do need to understand His plan for us, and certainly, He does explain that in the Bible. Furthermore, this is why the writing is so masterful in the Bible. It is so that those who are willing to take the time to read the Bible can hear from G-d. In Isaiah 46:8-10, Isaiah quotes G-d:

> "Remember this, and be assured; recall it to mind, you wrongdoers. Remember the former things long past, for I am G-d and there is no other; *I am* G-d and there is no one like Me, declaring the end from the beginning, and from ancient times things which have not been done, saying 'My plan will be established, and I will accomplish all My good pleasure';"

Surely G-d has a plan, and it is for our good. Not only has He explained His plan in the Bible, but He has also prophesied elements of it in advance so that we could know for certain that it is G-d who is at work as we see His plan unfolding. We do wrong when we discount G-d's message to us in the Bible or fail to take notice of what He has been doing in history. In short, He wants us to find Him, and He wants to bless us. But we have to care. We have to be willing to shift our gaze from whatever it is that is consuming us and turn to G-d to follow Him.

part two

SACRIFICIAL ATONEMENT IN THE TORAH

5

ABRAHAM AND ISAAC

The story of G-d asking Abraham to sacrifice Isaac is famous. For those of us who love the Bible, we have heard this story multiple times. Perhaps you have become numbed to the jaw-dropping element of this story. Do you remember the very first time you heard this story, perhaps as child? It is shocking. How could G-d ask any father to kill his own child? Abraham, of course, was caught off guard by G-d; but when G-d came through at the last moment with the substitutionary ram, he was elated. Abraham was so relieved and overjoyed that he immediately named the place where he sacrificed the ram. In fact, he named it a sentence: "the L-rd will see." It is unusual for a location to be given a full sentence for its name. But Abraham was so thankful that he wanted to memorialize G-d's gracious act by giving this name to the place where it happened.

Actually, this story is even more shocking than if G-d called on you to take the life of your child, because Isaac's birth was a miracle. Isaac was a gift from G-d. In fact, Isaac was not only a gift to Abraham and Sarah, but also to the whole world.

Many years earlier, when G-d first approached Abraham and called on him to leave his home and his family in Mesopotamia, he was seventy-five years old.[43] Accompanying him were his wife, Sarah, and his nephew, Lot. Sarah was ten years younger than Abraham.[44] She was barren,[45] and they had never been able to have a child. At the time of their departure, their names were actually Abram and Sarai. G-d would later change their names to Abraham and Sarah, signifying that their lives had changed on a fundamental level.

Abraham grew up in the heart of the ancient world as a member of a pagan family.[46] G-d called him out of that existence to a new life by first having him leave the city of Haran and head southwest to the land of Canaan. But more importantly, G-d was not just calling Abraham away from the life he knew in the ancient world; G-d was calling him to a new life in which G-d would reveal Himself to Abraham, bless him, and use him to play a very important role. Abraham's role was to father a nation which would become a key part of G-d's long-term plan to reach the spiritually lost people of this world. In the words of G-d: "by your descendants all the nations of the earth shall be blessed;"[47]

However, Sarah was barren. To father first a family, and ultimately a people, you have to start with the first one. But Abraham and Sarah had none. Of course, that is not a problem for G-d, who gives life.

---

[43] Gen. 12:4.

[44] Gen. 17:17.

[45] Gen. 11:30.

[46] Josh. 24:2.

[47] Gen. 12:3; 18:18; 22:18; 26:4; 28:14.

G-d promised Abraham and Sarah a son. But then a number of years went by and there was still no baby. So Abraham came up with a plan to help G-d. Namely, he thought he would take matters into his own hands and have a baby with Sarah's servant, Hagar. But G-d did not direct him to do that. Furthermore, it would have never been G-d's plan for Abraham to breach his marriage. Yet, Abraham went ahead with his plan and sure enough, along came Ishmael.

G-d allowed Abraham to make his mistake and to suffer the consequences. Ishmael was not G-d's choice to begin the people who would be His vehicle to bless mankind. Eventually Hagar and Ishmael were asked to leave, and they headed east.

In all, it took twenty-five years from the time G-d first made the promise to Abraham and Sarah to have a baby until the time the baby came. Abraham was one hundred and Sarah was ninety when Isaac was born. Their bodies were old, but with G-d's help, they had a baby boy.[48]

Why did G-d make them wait until they were this old before He fulfilled His promise and gave them a son? There are multiple reasons, but for our purposes, we will mention only one. Namely, G-d waited to the point that there could be no confusion. In every other case, when a young woman is pregnant, we know how it happened. But in the case of Abraham and Sarah, for the first time ever, their pregnancy was different. G-d intervened and enabled Abraham and Sarah to conceive, and He wants us to know that. Thus, He waited this long so that no one could deny that it was a miracle.

A number of years later, we come to Genesis 22. G-d said to Abraham: "Take your son, your only son whom you love, Isaac, and go to the land of Moriah; and offer him there as a burnt offering on one of the mountains of which I will tell

---

[48] Gen. 17:17; 18:9-15.

you."[49] This command would have made no sense at all. Why would G-d ever ask this of any father? But in this case, it was even more bewildering. Isaac was a unique, important, G-d-given child. This interaction had to catch Abraham off guard. But Abraham knew that G-d's ways are different from our ways, and that we don't always understand what G-d is doing. He also knew that G-d is good and G-d is trustworthy. Furthermore, Abraham learned his lesson the last time he tried to take matters into his own hands; so this time he chose to simply obey and do whatever G-d told him to do.

Hence, Genesis 22 goes on to record the details of Abraham going on a three-day journey with Isaac, two young men, and a donkey to the place where G-d told him to go. They took everything necessary for Abraham to offer Isaac as a sacrifice: wood for the fire, some kind of rope or cord to bind Isaac, and a knife to take his life. When they got close, the father and son finished the journey without the donkey and the two young men. While they walked the rest of the way, Isaac carried the wood, and he said: "Behold the fire and the wood, but where is the lamb for the burnt offering?"[50] Perhaps they had made burnt offerings before, and they always took a lamb with them. Or perhaps Isaac was aware of the pagan practice of child sacrifice, and he wondered if he was to be the sacrifice. Although, that would make no sense as G-d is nothing like the manmade gods of the ancient world, and He would never want a human life to be taken for His sake.

Of course, we do not actually know what Isaac's thoughts were because they were not recorded in Genesis. But Abraham's response was: "G-d will see to the sheep for His

---

[49] Gen. 22:2.
[50] Gen. 22:7.

burnt offering, my son."[51] (Another translation is: "G-d will provide for Himself the lamb for the burnt offering, my son."[52]) The meaning of Abraham's answer is somewhat vague; and that makes sense, since Abraham did not know exactly what was going to happen. But his answer does convey that G-d would be involved in whatever was going to happen, and that G-d can be trusted.

Once they got to their destination, Abraham built an altar and arranged the wood for the fire. Next, it appears as though Isaac accepted being the sacrifice, as Abraham was able to bind him and lay him on the wood. Then, trusting in G-d, Abraham raised the knife and was poised to do the deed, when the L-rd spoke from heaven and told him to stop. At that point, Abraham looked up and saw a ram caught by its horns in a thicket. Abraham then set Isaac free and offered the ram in his place. Abraham was overjoyed. In addition, G-d was pleased; and no doubt, Isaac was overjoyed as well.

*   *   *   *   *

It is understandable that Abraham would offer a burnt offering to G-d. It would only make sense for him to worship G-d and praise Him for His goodwill toward man and His plan to rescue the people of the world.[53] In addition, Abraham would have also offered the sacrifice to thank G-d for the honor of playing a role in G-d's plan and to dedicate himself to fulfilling that role.

---

[51] Gen. 22:8 from: Adele Berlin and Marc Zvi Brettler, eds., *The Jewish Study Bible*, 2nd ed. (New York, NY: Oxford University Press, 2005, 2014) 43.

[52] Gen. 22:8 from: *The Book of Genesis*, translation and commentary by Rabbi A. J. Rosenberg (Brooklyn: The Judaica Press, 1993) 256.

[53] Ps. 67:2.

What does not make any sense is why G-d would call for Abraham to offer Isaac as the sacrifice. What must the journey to Mount Moriah have been like for Abraham? There must have been a lot of silence. He had three days to ponder why this was happening. Of course, in the end, it did not happen. Once G-d provided the ram, Abraham's crisis was over. But it does not say that G-d ever provided Abraham with an explanation for why G-d picked Isaac to be a sacrifice in the first place.

Sometime prior to this event, Abraham had an interaction with G-d over His judgement of the cities of Sodom and Gomorrah. In that interaction, Abraham learned about justice and how G-d needed to judge sin. Then he saw how G-d spared his nephew, Lot, and evacuated Lot and his family out of Sodom. Certainly, Isaac was not like the wicked people of Sodom. So why was G-d calling for Isaac to die?

The point was not that G-d was calling for Isaac to die, but rather that He was calling for Isaac to die *as a sacrifice*. G-d picked Isaac to be the sacrifice because he was not like the wicked people of Sodom, for a sinful person cannot be a sacrifice. When a sinner perishes, they must serve their own sentence. Their death cannot cover another; it can only pay for their moral debt. But if a righteous person were to die, their death could pay the price for the sins of another.

Of course, Isaac was not actually righteous. Oh, relative to the rapists of Sodom, he was. But compared to G-d, Isaac was not. For example, later on in life, he and his wife each picked a different son to be their favorites, and there was conflict. As the leader of his family, the responsibility for this unhealthy dynamic fell on him. Thus, as a father, he was imperfect and people got hurt. He fell short of the righteousness of G-d. The point is that Isaac was picked to be the sacrifice symbolically, not literally.

So the question becomes: What is the meaning of G-d's symbology in the selection of Isaac to be the sacrifice? Again, the answer to this question is not given in the narrative in Genesis chapter 22. Rather, it may be the case that this outrageous event is essentially a puzzle piece, and it needs to be fit alongside other events in the Hebrew Bible in order for it to make sense. However, based on Genesis chapter 22, we can say a few things. For one, we can say that the sacrificial death of Isaac symbolizes something important, and that somehow sacrificial death is an element in G-d's plan for humanity. Furthermore, based on the way Abraham stated twice that G-d Himself would provide or see to the sacrifice, we can deduce that G-d would be the one who would one day provide the sacrifice to pay the price for human sin.

Also, we can learn from Abraham's example in this passage. He responded to G-d's command in utter faith. He was willing to sacrifice his precious child because he trusted in G-d's promises, goodness, and wisdom. Sure enough, G-d came through, and Abraham was overjoyed. Surely G-d was pleased with Abraham's faith. We should follow Abraham's example and place our faith in G-d's provision for us.

6

THE PASSOVER

The subject of Passover was introduced earlier in chapter 1 of this book, where the question was raised: Why did the Jewish people, who were the victims, need to sacrifice lambs? In that event, G-d was setting the Jews free from a horrid and long-term occurrence of oppression. It was so bad that they were groaning, literally. Finally, they reached the point where they cried out for help. G-d heard their cries, and He acted to deliver them,[54] for this is who G-d is. He cares about our plights, and He rescues us.

There ensued a conflict between G-d and Pharaoh. Pharaoh was considered to be a god by his Egyptian subjects. In fact, the Egyptians were quite religious, and they worshipped a large pantheon of pagan deities. In the ancient world, life was tenuous as famine, disease, war, and even attacks from wild beasts were constant threats. Survival was at the forefront of everyone's mind. Thus, people fabricated

---

[54] Ex. 2:23-25.

gods for themselves for the purpose of coping with these life-threatening circumstances. Of course, some years there would be plenty of rain and a good harvest; but other years there would be a drought and people would die. Thus, they surmised that the gods were capricious and undependable. Furthermore, the gods they made up were not like G-d; they were morally compromised like humans. Their idea was to appease the gods in order to gain things like rain, children, a good harvest, and victory in battle.

There were two main problems with ancient religion. Number one, their gods were not real. For example, the sun is not a god; it is a star. So, their gods did not exist and therefore could not come to their rescue. Number two, the worship practices people made up to appease their gods were depraved. These practices included things like child sacrifice and temple prostitution, which were immoral and abhorrent to G-d.

The conflict between G-d and Pharaoh consisted of a series of ten plagues. Prior to inflicting some of the plagues on the Egyptians, G-d first sent Moses to speak to Pharaoh and request that he let the Jews go and worship in the wilderness. In addition, Moses warned Pharaoh that if he would not let them leave, G-d would bring a plague down upon Egypt. Yet, Pharaoh was very stubborn and he would not let them go. Hence, a plague would come.

In the first plague, G-d turned the water of the Nile into blood. The Nile was very important to the Egyptians. In many ways, it was their source of life. But G-d was greater, and He turned this river, in which they drowned Jewish baby boys, into blood. In the next plague, He caused an unbelievable number of frogs to emerge from the Nile. They were everywhere. You could not turn around without stepping on one. When Pharaoh met with Moses, he said please, have your G-d remove these frogs; and so G-d did. The frogs on land all died and no new frogs emerged from the Nile. But the problem was not completely over, as there were mounds of dead frogs and the air became foul. Nonetheless, Pharoah was emboldened and rescinded his promise to let the Jewish people go.

This dance went on for some time, and the plagues came one after the other. It appears that in most cases, the plagues only fell upon the Egyptians and not the Jews. For instance, in Exodus 9:1-7, it says that a severe disease struck all the Egyptian livestock, but not a single Jewish animal perished. G-d was willing to dance this dance with Pharaoh, which was prolonged by Pharaoh's stubbornness. The length and breadth of their conflict provided G-d with an opportunity to firmly establish that He was the one true G-d and that the Egyptian gods were imposters. In fact, the conflict lasted so long that the news spread far and wide across the ancient world and people started to see who G-d is. Furthermore, the real G-d is the G-d the people of the world needed, as it is He who stands above creation and can deliver from calamity. In fact, in each of these plagues, G-d was demonstrating that He is in control of nature. So G-d was accomplishing two things in this event. First, He was setting the Jews free from slavery. Second, He was revealing Himself to the ancient world. For G-d wanted the Gentile peoples of the world to hear about Him, and not just so that they would be scared to harm the Jews; He also wanted the Gentiles to find out about Him so that they could believe in Him for their own good.[55]

When it comes to the tenth and most severe plague, G-d changes course. Here He has Moses not only issue a warning to Pharaoh and the Egyptians, but He also has Moses issue the same warning to the Jews! Pharaoh could avert the plague by letting the Jews go, whereas the Jews were offered a different

---

[55] Ex. 9:18-21; 12:38.

method to avert judgement. Of course, Pharaoh said no to G-d, but the Jews obeyed and were exempted from judgement. The ritual details appear in Exodus chapter 12. Each household had to select a one-year-old, unblemished, male lamb or goat on the tenth of the month. (If the household was small, they could share a lamb with another family.) Four days later, they were to kill the animal and put some of its blood on the two doorposts and the lintel above the doorway. Then they were to roast the animal whole (without breaking any of its bones) over fire and eat it that night. They were also to eat unleavened bread and bitter herbs. Any meat left over was to be burned in the fire the following morning. They were to eat it in haste, fully clothed, and with staff in hand. In other words, they would be leaving swiftly following the events that would take place that night.

Sadly, the L-rd passed through the land that night, and the firstborn son of each Egyptian family, including the firstborn of their animals, lost their lives. However, wherever G-d saw the blood on the doorframes, He would pass over those houses and the inhabitants would be safe. This event was so significant that G-d called for the Jews to memorialize it as an annual celebration from that point forward. Also, from then on, they were to start their calendar with that month being the first month of the year.

Surely death came that night in Egypt. Pharaoh was finally broken, and he released the Jews.[56] Again, the Egyptians believed that Pharaoh was a god, and so was his son. Perhaps even Pharaoh believed it. But those beliefs took a blow when Pharaoh's son perished. The king and the nation were learning who the real G-d is. Of course, this pharaoh was full of murder and evil. He regrouped and sent his army after the Jews some days later. In Exodus 14:5, it says that Pharaoh

---

[56] Ex. 12:32.

and his officers did not want to lose the free labor the Jews provided as slaves. How utterly arrogant. This set the stage for the final blow.

As the Egyptian army approached, the Jews were caught between the army and the Red Sea with no path of escape. The Jews were terrified.[57] However, G-d was not caught off guard, as He proceeded to suspend the laws of nature and open a pathway for the Jews through the Red Sea. But when the Egyptian army chased after them, their chariots' wheels did not do well on the floor of the Red Sea and it was chaotic. Then G-d caused the pent-up waters to come crashing down and the entire army drowned. Game, set, and match. G-d had singlehandedly defeated the Egyptian army.

At this point, G-d had demonstrated, in every way that would have been relevant in the ancient world, who He was. Namely, He was the one true, all-powerful, creator G-d. Exodus chapter 14 concludes by saying that as the Jews looked upon the bodies of the Egyptian soldiers that washed up on the beach, they believed in G-d, and they were ready to listen to His chosen leader, Moses.

* * * * *

Now let us consider more deeply our original question of why G-d called for each Jewish family to offer up a blood sacrifice lest they suffer judgement. On its face, this does not make any sense, for the Jews were the victims of this massive event of slavery and oppression, not the perpetrators. Clearly, G-d was trying to get the Jews' attention. Furthermore, G-d called for the ceremony of Passover to be performed once a year in perpetuity. He is still trying to get the Jews' attention.

---

[57] Ex. 14:10.

The crux of the matter is that the Jews were still sinners even though they were innocent victims of this historic crime. For, they each struggled with same sins as everyone else: lying, selfishness, gossiping, stealing, withholding forgiveness, and so on. Also, at some point in their 430-year-long stay in Egypt, they forgot about G-d. In Exodus 14:10, as Pharaoh chased them, it says that they "cried out to the L-rd." But this was after they had become reacquainted with G-d. At first, in Exodus 2:24, it just says: "they cried out." It does not add to whom. Of course, it would only be natural for them to have forgotten about G-d; that is what we do. The Jews were guilty in the same way that anyone who grows up in a loving family and then moves away and forgets about their parents would be. Furthermore, they were guilty in much the same way as Esau, who did not value the things of G-d. Also, as stated earlier, the Egyptians were quite religious. Consequently, the Jews were exposed to their religious activities; and sure enough, eventually the Jews began to worship the false gods of the Egyptians.[58] Thus, the Jews betrayed G-d.

However, G-d is not like us. He is forgiving. He is also an order of magnitude higher than us in intelligence. He knows that what we need more than deliverance from suffering in this life, even great suffering, is salvation from judgement in eternity. This is why He included this detail that seems incongruous. He wanted the Jews to see that they, too, were guilty, and that He had a plan to provide atonement for their sins.

---

[58] Josh. 24:14; Ezek. 20:1-10.

7

THE TABERNACLE FURNISHINGS

The purpose of the Temple was not to be a home for G-d. In fact, even as the priests brought the Ark of the Covenant into the inner sanctuary of the new Temple, Solomon declared that the Temple was not actually G-d's house or home.[59] G-d does not need a shelter. However, for our sake, He was there! He manifested Himself in the form of a cloud that filled the inner sanctuary.[60] The purpose of the Temple was to serve as the place where G-d dwelt among His people.

The layout of the Temple is similar to its earlier, mobile version, the Tabernacle. In Exodus chapters 25 through 31, G-d prescribed in precise detail the design of the Tabernacle, including the layout, the materials that were to be used, and the associated utensils, furniture, and priestly garments that

---

[59] 1 Kin. 8:27.
[60] 1 Kin. 8:10.

were to be produced. These instructions were so detailed that they left no room for any creative input by man. The reason for G-d's rigidity in this case was because G-d was prescribing the process by which man may approach Him. Of course, we have long since forfeited the right to have any say in this matter, by virtue of our rebellion. In addition, we are so profoundly spiritually confused or blind that we are inadequate to offer an opinion on this matter. In short, the only way to come to G-d is His way. Thank G-d that He has provided us with one.

It turns out that when it comes to interior decorating, G-d is a minimalist. The Tabernacle was a large, open air enclosure in which a courtyard surrounded an inner tent consisting of two rooms. The Outer Courtyard contained two pieces of furniture, the first room of the inner tent contained three, and the innermost room contained one. That's it. Perhaps G-d did not want any religious clutter in the meeting place He prescribed for His people. In fact, G-d carefully selected each of the design elements of the Tabernacle for a reason. Namely, He was trying to communicate a message in the design of how we can come to Him and come into His presence.

One of the important details of the Tabernacle consisted of the doorways. There were three of them: the doorway into the Tabernacle, the doorway into the Holy Place (the first room of the inner tent), and the doorway into the Holy of Holies (the innermost room). The word 'holy' means separate. G-d is separate from us. He is righteous and pure, and we are not. We are morally unfit to be in His presence. Hence, G-d double-used the word for separate when He named the inner sanctuary 'the Holy of Holies' to make sure we got the message. The reality of the separation between G-d and us is further communicated by the veil blocking the doorway to the Holy of Holies.

The doorway to the Tabernacle faced east. This makes sense in that when Adam and Eve were removed from G-d's presence in the Garden of Eden following their act of rebellion, they exited on the east side. Thus, to return to G-d, one must come back to the west. Further, the inner tent was on the west half of the Tabernacle, and the Holy of Holies was on the west side of the inner tent. Jewish people could enter the courtyard of the Tabernacle, but only the priests could enter the Holy Place. Beyond that, only the High Priest could enter the Holy of Holies, and only once a year, on the Day of Atonement.

Upon entering the Tabernacle courtyard, there were two pieces of furniture: an altar and a laver. The Bronze Altar is where the sacrifices were offered. This was the first piece of furniture encountered upon entering through the doorway. Exodus 20:25 stipulates that the altar was to be constructed of uncut stones. The Jews were only to use stones they found lying on the ground in the state G-d formed them. The message here is that in our state of moral imperfection, we are incapable of contributing anything towards the payment required for our sins.[61] In Exodus 20:25, it says that if the Jews were to use a tool on the stones, they would "profane it (the altar)." In addition, the animals prescribed for the sacrifices had to be unblemished, which symbolized their being pure and thus fit to pay the price for our imperfection. To be sure, when a sinner dies, they can only pay the price for their own sins, not anyone else's. Of course, the process of offering a sacrifice began with the spectacle of slaughtering an innocent animal. Perhaps G-d is trying to get our attention, and He is telling us that all we can do is simply look down in solemn

---

[61] Of course, there were different kinds of animal sacrifices, but the most important ones were the sin offerings. (Alfred Edersheim, *The Temple: Its Ministry and Services,* updated ed. (Peabody, Massachusetts: Hendrickson Publishers, Inc., 1994) 94.)

humility as another living being dies in our place. There is no room for taking credit for our right-standing before G-d; rather, it can only be received as a gift from our loving heavenly Father.

The laver was a bronze basin filled with water which the priests were to use to ceremonially wash their hands and feet. As it says in Exodus 30:17-21:

> And the L-rd spoke to Moses, saying, "You shall also make a laver of bronze, with its base of bronze, for washing; and you shall put it between the tent of meeting and the altar, and you shall put water in it. And Aaron and his sons shall wash their hands and their feet from it; when they enter the tent of meeting, they shall wash with water, that they may not die; or when they approach the altar to minister by offering up in smoke a fire sacrifice to the L-rd. So they shall wash their hands and their feet, that they may not die; and it shall be a perpetual statue for them, for Aaron and his descendants throughout their generations."

The point of the Bronze Laver is consistent with the message that G-d has for us with the altar. It is also dramatic. If a priest tried to either enter the inner tent or offer up sacrifices on the altar without first washing their hands and feet, they would die. Of course, this was not hard to do, and the priests were in no danger so long as they simply followed protocol. But again, the message is that we are separate from G-d. We are distinctly different and unworthy to enter His presence. This is the case for every human being, even the descendants of Aaron, the priests. Needless to say, the water was just water. The ceremonial washing did not magically transform them and somehow make them acceptable to G-d. It was just symbolic of how we are utterly unfit to be in G-d's presence and in need of an actual spiritual cleansing of our souls.

In the Holy Place, there were three more pieces of furniture: the Altar of Incense, the Golden Lampstand, and the Table of Showbread, upon which sat the Bread of Presence. These pieces were all made out of gold. Of course, inside the innermost room, the Holy of Holies, was the most famous piece of furniture, the Ark of the Covenant.

The Table of Showbread had twelve loaves of bread placed on top which were replaced every Sabbath. The twelve loaves represent the twelve tribes of Israel. The bread symbolizes G-d's care and provision for His people, both for their physical needs and their spiritual needs.[62] Of course, being G-d's chosen people is nothing short of an absolute honor. It is also a great responsibility. G-d's attribute of faithfulness is on display in the Table of Showbread in that He will forever be faithful to the promises He made to Abraham regarding his descendants, the Jewish people.

The Golden Lampstand is the sole light source in the inner tent. On one hand, the priests needed it so that they could see. But on the other hand, it has a symbolic meaning. Indeed, G-d imbued each of the six pieces of Tabernacle furniture with meaning. The lamp had a center shaft with three branches on each side, and thus there were seven flames. It was an oil lamp, the fuel of which came from pure olive oil. It was to be constantly replenished so that it would never go out. The message here appears to be man's need for continual spiritual illumination from G-d. We are profoundly spiritually confused and lost, and only with G-d's personal assistance can

---

[62] Deut. 8:3.

any of us grasp spiritual truth. But He is there perpetually to provide understanding to anyone who turns to Him with an open mind.

The Altar of Incense is special, based on the location it was given in the Tabernacle. As it says in Exodus 30:6: "And you shall put this altar in front of the veil that is near *the ark* of the testimony, in front of the mercy seat that is over the ark of the testimony, where I will meet you." This altar was to be placed close to the presence of G-d, just on the other side of the veil. A specific combination of spices was required for the incense, the aroma of which wafted upwards as it burned on the altar. Even though man was not permitted beyond the veil, the aroma was able to permeate into the Holy of Holies as the inner tent would not have been airtight. However, G-d did not prescribe that the altar be placed there because He wanted to enjoy the fragrance. Rather, the incense is symbolic of something that is dear to G-d. In the Christian New Testament, it explicitly states that the aroma represents the prayers of G-d's people.[63] We also see this association between incense and the prayers of G-d's people in the Hebrew Bible in Psalm 141:2. Of course, G-d is not interested in hearing His people recite formulaic, religious prayers, and He did not call for the Jews to approach Him in this way in the Hebrew Bible. He is a real person who wants to hear from real people speaking from their hearts. We do see G-d responding positively to these kinds of prayers in the Hebrew Bible.

There are many instances of personal prayers in the Hebrew Bible. One example would be when Hannah cried out to G-d in the midst of her pain. Hannah was not a VIP in Jewish society. She was one of the two wives of Elkanah. But she was important to G-d, who answered her prayer and gave

---

[63] Rev. 5:8.

her a son.[64] Of course, when the baby came, Hannah prayed again, only this time she spoke words of joy and praise. Another example of someone praying in the Hebrew Bible would be King David, who wrote half of the psalms. His psalms were prayers that were both personal and poetic. For example, in Psalm 3, David prayed for deliverance from his enemies, and in Psalm 139, David worshiped G-d as he marveled at G-d's deep personal love for him. In Psalm 51, David addressed another matter. David had committed adultery with Bathsheba. Then he attempted to cover it up by having her husband, Uriah, murdered. Upon being confronted by the prophet Nathan, David came to understand the gravity of his sin. In this psalm, he confessed his sin to G-d. Then he asked G-d to extend him compassion, and to not cast him out of His presence.

There are many other examples of personal prayers in the Hebrew Bible, but the point is that this piece of furniture, the Altar of Incense, provides us with a glimmer of hope. Despite our state of moral corruption and unfitness to be in G-d's presence, He loves us anyway! He wants to hear from us, and He even finds our prayers to be a pleasing aroma.

This leaves us with one more room and one final piece of furniture. But first, let's consider some dimensions. The Tabernacle, Holy Place, and Table of Showbread were all two-to-one rectangles in terms of their lengths vs. their widths. The Holy of Holies, Altar of Incense, and Bronze Altar were all squares. In fact, the Holy of Holies was a cube with the dimensions 10:10:10 (where the units are cubits, in which one cubit equals approximately 18 inches). The Holy of Holies was the only design element that was a cube as the Altar of Incense was 1:1:2, and the Bronze Altar was 5:5:3 (where the final dimension is the height). The ark was a box that had the

---

[64] 1 Sam. 1:10-13.

dimensions 2.5:1.5:1.5. So, the Holy of Holies was the only cube, and the Ark of the Covenant was the only piece of furniture in which the length vs. width ratio was neither 2:1, nor square.[65] Considering how meaningful all of the elements in the Tabernacle are, it appears G-d is trying to get our attention and tell us that something very important is going on in the Holy of Holies with the Ark of the Covenant.

The ark was a wooden box that was covered in gold, inside and out. On top of the ark was a solid gold lid or cover. The Hebrew word for this cover is 'kappōret'. Kappōret is translated differently in different versions of the Bible, but it means a place or an object of propitiation or atonement. Hence, for example, in the New American Standard Bible (NASB) it is translated as "mercy seat ." On each end of the cover, there was a cherub. The two cherubim face each other, with their wings extended upward and forward over the gold cover. Although they faced each other, they looked downward. The cover and two cherubs were all sculpted or hammered out of the same piece of gold.

Inside the ark were placed the two replacement stone tablets upon which G-d Himself inscribed the ten commandments. (Moses broke the first set when he came down from Mt. Sinai and witnessed the disgusting behavior of his countrymen.) In the Christian New Testament, in Hebrews 9:4, it further states that a gold jar of manna and Aaron's rod that budded were also in the ark (which correlates with Exodus 16:32-34 and Numbers 17:10 (25), respectively).[66]

---

[65] No dimensions were given in the Hebrew Bible for either the Bronze Laver or the Golden Lampstand.

[66] It should be noted that in Josephus' history book, *The Antiquities of the Jews*, only the stone tablets are mentioned as being in the ark. (Josephus Flavius, *The Antiquities of the Jews*, 3.6.5 (138) from: *The Works of Josephus*, Complete and Unabridged, New

Manna was the food G-d miraculously provided the Jews while they wandered for forty years in the desert. Of course, the Jews were relegated to wandering in the desert due to their lack of faith and refusal to enter the promised land. Then they followed that up by complaining about the manna and saying ". . . we loathe this miserable food."[67] Aaron's rod was a staff that miraculously budded overnight when the staffs of the other eleven tribes remained mere dead pieces of wood, thereby indicating G-d's selection of the house of Aaron alone to be His priests. G-d had already made this selection, but some of the Jews were jealous and they grumbled and rebelled against His choice of Aaron. Therefore, G-d responded by judging the leaders of the rebellion and performing this miracle to make it abundantly clear that He selected Aaron and his descendants to be His human representatives. Of course, it is G-d's right to choose whoever He wants to be His priests.

In Exodus 25:16, the ark is called "the ark of the testimony ." The Hebrew word for testimony is ʻēdût. It is a legal term stemming from the root word ʻûd, which means to bear witness. Testimony is a good translation, and it means the statement of a witness or a piece of physical evidence that is used to establish the facts.

Again, the cherubs are not looking at each other; they are looking down at the ark containing the testimony or evidence. Of course, the cherubs were just sculptures, whereas G-d presence (between the two cherubs) was real.[68] However, these two statues of angels represent a greater reality. Namely, they represent the "myriads upon myriads"[69] of angels who

---

Updated Edition, trans. William Whiston, A.M. (Peabody, MA: Hendrickson Publishers, Inc., 2009) 88.)

[67] Num. 21:4.
[68] Ex. 25:22.
[69] Dan. 7:10.

attend to G-d and play a behind-the-scenes role in the interactions between G-d and man. These angels see the spectacle that is us. They have witnessed the great events of evil down through the ages, but they also see you and me in our daily lives. They hear the words that come out of our mouths and they see what we do. In addition, they can see G-d, and they witness His words and deeds. Ever since our foreparents, Adam and Eve, were removed from G-d's presence in the garden, we have no longer been able to see G-d, and our understanding of Him is weak. But the angels do see G-d, and in Him, they witness righteousness. Thus, as the two cherubs representing the vast angelic realm peer down upon the evidence of our sins in the ark, they understand that there must be justice, and they are awaiting G-d's ruling. So, the scene that is taking place in the Holy of Holies is a court trial. To be precise, this particular trial taking place in the Tabernacle is only for the sins committed by G-d's chosen people, the Jews. It is the evidence of their rebellion against G-d that is on display in the ark.

Needless to say, the evidence is damning. The Jews are guilty, and justice is required. The sentence is death. This goes all the way back to Adam and Eve. When Adam and Eve rebelled, first they were separated from G-d and taken out of paradise to experience life in a broken world. Then they died. The sentence remains the same for the Jews. Thus, in this trial, the accused are proven guilty and a sentence of death is required. However, there is a very unusual element in this courtroom. There is a "mercy seat"!

In G-d's infinite wisdom, He is able to see to it that justice is not compromised, and yet that mercy is granted! He is able to accomplish these seemingly conflicting goals by having a substitute take on the punishment that is due the Jewish people. Hence, once a year, on the Day of Atonement, a bull and a goat are put to death. After each slaying, the high priest brings the blood into the Holy of Holies and presents it to the L-rd by following a scripted service in which he sprinkles the blood on the east side of the top of the mercy seat and in front of the mercy seat.[70]

Thus, the angels, who have witnessed all the crimes and all the private sins committed throughout the ages, are beholding this unique court trial. They have been looking down upon the evidence, and now they are seeing blood being sprinkled on the cover of the ark, signifying that the sentence has been carried out. So, justice has been served and everything has been made right.

Or has it?

Of course, we all sense that despite the spectacle and the gravity of the high priest himself slaughtering innocent animals, entering the very presence of G-d, and performing all the rituals prescribed by G-d, something is still wrong. First of all, the sins of the Gentiles were not paid for on the Day of Atonement. Second, if everything was made right, why couldn't the Jewish people freely enter into G-d's presence and be with Him in the way that Adam and Eve were? For certainly, they were not welcome to do that at the conclusion of the ceremony. Thus, were the Jews' sins really paid for by the deaths of these animals? Or, were the deaths merely symbolic of a greater fulfillment by a substitute who G-d would one day provide and who actually could pay the price for the sins of mankind? Perhaps G-d instituted the Day of Atonement, with all of its intensity and graphic details, for the purpose of getting His people's attention, bringing to the forefront of their minds the gravity of their situation, and yet communicating that there was hope for a solution in Him.

---

[70] Lev. 16:1-19.

*   *   *   *   *

G-d is a great communicator. First and foremost, He speaks through the beautiful and profound writings in the Hebrew Bible. But He also speaks in other ways. He speaks through nature. He speaks through His actions in history. Furthermore, He uses symbolism and imagery to teach us lessons. This is the case with the Tabernacle and the Temple. Let's try to clear our minds and look upon this imagery with fresh eyes, and see if we can hear from G-d.

The Tabernacle is called the "tent of meeting" in the Hebrew Bible. This is a very important and special place where G-d and man are to come together. What is G-d saying to us about the health of our relationship with Him and the condition of man in general? Does this imagery communicate that things are basically OK, but that perhaps there is some room for us to improve and make some adjustments in regards to our beliefs and conduct? Or, is G-d saying through this imagery that yes, there is a problem, but it has been solved through the laws and religious practices set forth in the Torah? Thus, the Jews were able to experience the communion with G-d that took place in the Tabernacle. Surely, neither of these answers is correct. Rather, what G-d is communicating through the imagery of the Tabernacle is that we are in a dire situation. Our relationship with Him is fractured, we are deserving of judgement, and we are awaiting sentencing. Our only hope is for a perfect substitute to shed their blood and pay the awful price of justice in our place.

Thus, it is not the case that the Tabernacle and the ceremonies of Judaism make up the solution to the problem between G-d and man. Rather, these things are symbols that portend a solution. All of the slain bulls and goats and all of the blood sprinkled on the mercy seat down through the ages communicated that G-d has a plan to take care of our problem.

Specifically, He has a plan to restore us to a state of worthiness so that we can enter His presence and have a relationship with Him in the way that Adam and Eve once did. When Adam and Eve were with Him in the garden, they did not perform any religious rituals. It was just the three of them; and they spent time with each other, enjoyed conversation, and no doubt, expressed love towards each other. Certainly, this form of meeting between G-d and man is what the outcome of G-d's plan to restore man will look like, not the strained, impersonal, ritualistic form of relating that took place in the tent of meeting.

But again, before we can enter into a personal relationship with G-d, the price for our sins must be paid. G-d is not going to say, "Oh well, let's just forget it; it's OK." We have said and done things that are not OK. G-d cannot and will not compromise justice. Therefore, our only hope is to have a substitute pay the price for our sins. If we are to pay that price ourselves, then we will die and never experience a love relationship with our heavenly Father. Of course, the deaths of all those sacrificial animals never actually paid the price of justice. After all, how could the death of a goat make up for my vile sin? The sacrifices just painted a vivid picture that we have a problem that is beyond our ability to solve. We need a savior from G-d, who actually can stand in as a substitute and take on the price of our sins.

8

THE DAY OF ATONEMENT

Leviticus chapters 16 and 23:26-32 prescribe the rituals of the Day of Atonement. In fact, it would be best for you to read those passages first and then return to this chapter.

Leviticus chapter 16 goes into fine detail about the rituals that were to be performed on this day. Similar to the Tabernacle, in which G-d prescribed the elements down to the minutest detail, so too did G-d establish the elements of the Day of Atonement with no room for human innovation or addition. Again, the reason is that we have sinned, and atonement must be made in order for us to be able to come into G-d's presence. Therefore, atonement is vitally important, and it must be made correctly. This is why G-d scripted the Day of Atonement and did not leave it up to us to figure out how to atone for our sins.

The main players in the ceremony on the Day of Atonement were the High Priest, two male goats, a bull, and

G-d Himself. The Jewish people were there, but they did not participate. They only watched. Even though the symbolism behind the rituals was very deep, this was not a pleasant event to attend like a play or a concert. This was a grave day as the purpose of this event was for another to be executed in their place.

The proceedings started out with the High Priest bathing and putting on special linen holy garments. Next, two identical goats were brought before him, and he cast lots to select one goat to be sacrificed and the other to be set free in the wilderness. Then he slaughtered the bull for his own sins and those of his household. Following that, he took some coals from the Altar of Incense along with two handfuls of finely ground sweet incense and entered through the veil into the Holy of Holies. Once inside, he threw the incense on the coals (which were in a firepan), and a cloud of incense formed above the mercy seat. Next, he dipped his finger in the container holding the bull's blood and proceeded to sprinkle blood on the east side of the top of the mercy seat and in front of it. Then it was time for him to slaughter the goat that was selected to be sacrificed and bring its blood into the Holy of Holies to be sprinkled in the same way he sprinkled the bull's blood. Finally, the High Priest took some blood from both the bull and the goat and sprinkled it on the horns of the Bronze Altar.

These sprinklings of blood were sin offerings for the High Priest's sins and the sins of the people. Furthermore, the purpose of these sprinklings was also to "make atonement for the holy place."[71] Indeed, it was necessary for the tent of meeting to be cleansed from the moral filth of the people who had traversed its ground and interacted with its utensils and furnishings. Our sinfulness is a grave matter. G-d will not

---

[71] Lev. 16:16-20, 33.

allow sinful people to come close to Him, even to perform religious duties, without atonement being made first.

Next, we come to an unusual element in the Jewish religion: the other goat, who was set free. He had a name. It was 'ăzā'zēl.[72] The NASB translates this word as "scapegoat." But 'ăzā'zēl can be interpreted in different ways, and there is some difference of opinion as to the correct interpretation. Much is written on this. Please look it up if you are curious. What is agreed upon is what happened to this goat. Following the sacrifices, the High Priest placed his hands on the head of the scapegoat and symbolically transferred all the sins of the Jewish people onto it. Then the goat would be led out into the wilderness such that he would never come back.

Afterward, there were some more rituals, including ceremonial washings, burnt offerings, and taking the dead bull and the dead goat outside of the camp and burning their remains.

These are the basic ceremonial elements that took place on the Day of Atonement. There are four main points to be learned from the Day of Atonement. The first one has to do with our current state of separation from G-d.

The High Priest was ostensibly the most pious person of the entire Jewish people. Yet, he was unwelcome and unworthy to come into the presence of G-d because of his moral filth. In verse 1, G-d starts off by reminding Aaron and the High Priests who would come after him of the tragedy of Nadab and Abihu. These two men are still famous today for their mistake. They didn't follow G-d's specific instructions regarding the Tabernacle and its rituals, and G-d took their lives on the spot. G-d is very serious about these things. It says in Leviticus chapter 10:1-2 that, like the High Priest, they also took a firepan of coals and placed incense on it. The result was

---

[72] Lev. 16:10.

that they were consumed in a fireball from the L-rd. It is not clear exactly which ritual they violated. It may be that they entered through the veil into G-d's presence without being called.

Thus, in chapter 16, verse 1, the message to the High Priests would have been loud and clear: "Do not change anything, and do not add anything. Do exactly what I tell you because you don't belong here, and it is dangerous for you to be in here." Upon entering through the veil, the High Priest had to first offer the incense and create a cloud over the mercy seat. So, even though he entered the Holy of Holies, there was still a cloud separating him from G-d. Then he would sprinkle the mercy seat with blood from the bull followed by the blood from the goat. Once he finished that, he had to immediately get out. It was not very dignified. But that is not G-d's fault. That is our fault. We have each lost our dignity through the sins we have committed and the dirt in our hearts.

On the day of Atonement, the Jewish people were called to step back from their everyday lives, take a moment, and think about where they stood before G-d. Whereas in Leviticus 16:1, the passage starts out with a caution to the High Priest to have his attitude right regarding his position before G-d, the passage in Leviticus 23 starts out by addressing the people to have their attitudes right, for they too were in a precarious position before the L-rd. In verses 27 through 32, G-d is speaking to Moses regarding the Jewish people, and He says:

> "On exactly the tenth day of this seventh month is the day of atonement; it shall be a holy convocation for you, and you shall humble your souls and present an offering by fire to the L-rd. You shall not do any work on this very day, for it is a Day of Atonement, to

make atonement on your behalf before the L-rd your G-d. If there is any person who does not humble himself on this very day, he shall be cut off from his people. As for any person who does any work on this very day, that person I will eliminate from among his people. You shall not do any work. It is to be a permanent statute throughout your generations in all your dwelling places. It is to be a Sabbath of complete rest for you, and you shall humble yourselves; on the ninth of the month at evening, from evening until evening, you shall keep your Sabbath."

Here G-d uses strong, direct language to call the people to be humble and to hold an additional Sabbath day. Humility is the opposite of arrogance. It means to appraise yourself in line with reality and not to think of yourself in relation to others as being more important than you are. Humility also applies to our attitude about ourselves in relation to G-d. It means to understand where we stand before G-d, which is that we are guilty.

The second point to be learned from the Day of Atonement is that G-d alone would provide for the Jews' atonement. Among all of the pieces of furniture and design elements of the Tabernacle and all of the ritual details of the Day of Atonement, there was nothing that was symbolic of the Jews contributing towards the payment for their crimes against G-d. They were mere spectators. It is similar to the moment when the Jews were standing between the Egyptian army and the Red Sea. No Jew would wield a sword against the Egyptians that day. G-d had placed a human leader, Moses, with them; and Moses lifted his staff and extended his hand over the sea. But it was G-d who actually defeated the

Egyptian army. Thus, in Exodus 14:13-14 we read: "Moses said to the people, "Do not fear! Stand by and see the salvation of the L-rd which He will accomplish for you today; for the Egyptians whom you have seen today, you will never see them again forever. The L-rd will fight for you while you keep silent." On the Day of Atonement, the Jews were again spectators and not participants. Yes, there was a human leader performing rituals, but really it was up to G-d to one day take care of everything regarding their atonement.

In addition, the requirement to hold a Sabbath on the Day of Atonement reinforced the Jews' need to trust G-d to provide atonement. Sabbath rest means refraining from labor and instead trusting in G-d to provide for your needs. In this case, they needed G-d to provide not for their physical needs, but rather for their spiritual need for forgiveness. They could not do any works to accomplish this for themselves. They had to rely on G-d to provide forgiveness for them, which He did symbolically on the Day of Atonement through the sacrificial goat and the scapegoat.

The third important point that is evident from the Hebrew Bible about the Day of Atonement is that something is missing. The Day of Atonement is incomplete. In fact, it falls far short of being a G-d-sized solution to the problem of sin that separates us from G-d. First, this day needed to be repeated every year. It was a temporary fix, not a permanent solution. Second, the High Priest only sprinkled blood on the east side of the top of the mercy seat. The sins of the Jewish people were still on display before the angels in this unique courtroom. Yes, the angels could see blood droplets along the periphery. But the blood did not cover the entire mercy seat which was the lid over the body of Jewish sin inside the ark. Therefore, it appears that the Jews were still in peril; their crimes were still not covered. Third, the sins that the sacrificial goat atoned for were only the unintentional, accidental sins of the Jewish people, not the volitional ones. The price of justice for those sins was not paid on the Day of Atonement![73] Thus, at the conclusion of each yearly Day of Atonement, every Jewish person should have felt uneasy. Their acceptance before G-d was not resolved by the rituals that took place on that day.

It is interesting that the High Priest was to enter the Holy of Holies from the east and place the blood on the east side of the mercy seat. Again, this detail appears to be a reference to Adam and Eve, who exited from G-d's presence to the east. The Jews are also connected to their progenitors in that just like Adam and Eve, they rebelled against G-d on a fundamental level, as proven by the specific pieces of evidence inside the Ark of the Covenant. In addition, just as one day Adam and Eve perished, so too the judicial sentence of death was carried out on the Day of Atonement. But G-d had the High Priest only sprinkle the east side of the mercy seat with the blood from the sacrificial animals. In other words, this ceremony was not intended to bring the Jews fully back into G-d's presence in the way that Adam and Eve once were. It was only a first step hinting at an eventual solution in which all the sins of man would be paid for. Of course, this fact is patently evident by the way the High Priest had to quickly exit from G-d's presence.

The fourth main lesson to be learned from the Day of Atonement is about the nature of atonement. Without atonement, there could be no reunion of G-d and man unless G-d were to waive justice. But He is not going to do that; for without justice, G-d would not be G-d.

In Genesis 4:10, G-d said to Cain: "What have you done? The voice of your brother's blood is crying to Me from the ground." How intrinsically true. There must be justice, and

---

[73] Heb. 9:7.

not simply justice for murder or sins of that degree. Even when we wound others with our words, those wounds are not insignificant, and they cry out to G-d for justice as well.[74]

The verb 'to make atonement' is the Hebrew word 'kāpar'. It is related to the following words: kappōret, which is the Hebrew word for mercy seat; kōper, which means a ransom payment; and kippūr, which is a noun that means atonement. Kippūr is the word used in the name of the holiday, Yom Kippur. Specifically, kāpar is derived from the noun, kōper. Thus, kāpar, or to make atonement, often means to pay a ransom or to redeem. Most of the usages in the Hebrew Bible of the word kāpar have to do with priests sprinkling the blood of sacrificial animals in order to provide redemption for worshippers.[75] In fact, the word kāpar is used in this sense fifteen times in Leviticus chapter 16.

It appears that there are two parts of atonement. Hence, there were two goats, who performed separate functions. The role of the sacrificial goat is obvious. He was to be a substitute and take the punishment for the people's sins. However, it is also obvious that the goat was merely symbolic. How could the death of a goat, or any other animal, pay the price for human sin? It cannot. On top of that, it would not be voluntary on the part of the goat. Wouldn't a substitute have to take on another's sentence voluntarily in order to satisfy justice?

But what is the other goat's role in atoning for sin? The scapegoat got to live but it was sent out, taking the sins of the people with it. This could mean that he took the guilt of their sins away. This interpretation would seem to agree with Psalm 103:12. But a better interpretation is that the scapegoat took

[74] Mt. 5:22.

[75] R. Laird Harris, Gleason L. Archer, Jr., and Bruce K. Waltke, eds., *Theological Wordbook of the Old Testament* (Chicago, Moody Press, 1980), 1:452-453.

the Jews' sins away in the sense that the people were set free from their sins. In other words, they would no longer have the capacity or the propensity to sin anymore. That interpretation would agree with the ritual for the cleansing of a leper in Leviticus 14:1-9. In that ritual there were similarly two birds: a sacrificial bird and a bird that was set free. The idea with the bird that was set free appears to be not that the bird flew away with the moral guilt of the leper, but that it flew away with the leprosy. In other words, the ritual meant that the leper was healed and the leprosy was not coming back.

Of course, like the sacrificial goat, the scapegoat was also symbolic. Oh, the goat was real, and it was really sent out, but the people's sins were not actually transferred onto him. The people's sins were still with them. Perhaps people tried harder not to sin around the Day of Atonement, but after a while, they fell right back into their sins. Arrogant people still thought too highly of themselves. People with short tempers still got upset easily. Gossips still fell prey to their sin, and so on. Therefore, the people needed to repeat the Day of Atonement the next year. Had the scapegoat actually taken their sins away, then they would not have sinned anymore, and there would have been no need for another Day of Atonement.

Thus, the Day of Atonement teaches us that there are two aspects of atonement. They include the payment for our guilt and the removal of our propensity to sin so that we can live righteously. Living this way entails not just our actions or what we do, but it also includes having a pure heart. Both of these aspects of atonement are necessary in order for us to be fit to enter G-d's presence. For, without the first aspect, justice would be compromised; and without the second one, we would turn heaven into a cesspool.

Again, there is a parallel between the Day of Atonement and the sentencing of Adam and Eve. Adam and Eve rebelled, became corrupt, and were no longer fit to be in G-d's presence.

Therefore, they were sent out or banished, and eventually they perished. How exactly did Adam and Eve become so altered that they were morally corrupt and unable to restore themselves? We don't know because G-d does not explain that in the Hebrew Bible. But what we do know is that Adam and Eve became morally corrupt, and we are exactly like them. We are not righteous; we are not anything like G-d. When the prophet Isaiah saw the L-rd in a vision, he immediately said "Woe is me, for I am ruined! because I am a man of unclean lips, and I live among a people of unclean lips."[76] That is the state we are in. To atone for our sins, a substitute must pay the price of death on our behalf, and our moral corruption must be removed from us such that we are fundamentally cleansed or changed. Only then can we return and enjoy a relationship with G-d in the way that Adam and Eve did at first. The purpose of the Day of Atonement was to bring this reality into focus, and even though it was apparent that the two goats were insufficient to provide atonement, there was always hope. For, the message of the Day of Atonement was that, one day, G-d would provide the real substitute.

* * * * *

As Israel was collapsing during the Roman siege, Rabbi Yochanan Ben Zakkai escaped from the Zealots inside Jerusalem, became Nasi (leader of the rabbis and the nation), gained approval by the Romans to continue the practice of Rabbinic Judaism, and established a new center of Judaism in the city of Yavneh. He responded to the destruction of the Temple both by providing a new understanding of atonement[77] and by making alterations to the rituals of the

---

[76] Isa. 6:5.

[77] Brian Tice, BS, MSci., *Reflecting on the Rabbis* (Grand Rapids, Michigan: MJR Press, 2017) 81-82.

Jewish festivals. These alterations enabled the festivals to go on without the Temple.[78] Indeed, his leadership was so impactful that Judaism still bears the imprint of his reforms today.

His determination to save Judaism is admirable, and his long-term impact is striking. However, his theological interpretation of atonement is subject to question. He is attributed as having said, "My son: be not grieved. We have another atonement as effective as this [Temple sacrifice system]. And what is it? It is acts of loving-kindness, as it is said: 'For I desire mercy, and not a sacrifice' [Hosea 6:6]" (*Avot d'Rabbi Nathan 4*).[79] However, Hosea 6:6 does not negate Leviticus 16 and the Day of Atonement. Certainly, G-d is pleased by our acts of kindness, and He does not desire the death of an animal substitute. Yet, this does not mean that our moral failures are atoned for by our acts of kindness. Atonement is not the subject of the book of Hosea; and nor does the word kāpar appear even one time in Hosea. Again, G-d provides atonement, we are mere spectators as another stands in for us to take on the sentence for our wrongdoings.

That is not to say that following G-d's moral law, worshipping only G-d, and treating other people with honesty and goodness are not important. Certainly, they are. Furthermore, the promise to the Jews for living by the Mosaic Law was protection and blessing upon blessing in this life.[80] Nonetheless, the Mosaic Law not only contained a moral law code for the Jewish people, but it also included the Day of Atonement and the ongoing practice of making sin offerings. That is because we are not perfect. The promise to the Jews for following the moral portion of the Mosaic Law was not

---

[78] Ibid., pp. 83-84.
[79] Ibid., p. 82.
[80] Deut. 29-30.

acceptance or the right to come into His presence. Atonement is required for that.

Another alternative to the Day of Atonement that has been suggested is repentance. For example, modern day rabbi Tovia Singer writes:

> Throughout the Jewish Scriptures, the prophets declared that repentance and charity are more pleasing to G-d for atonement than a blood sacrifice.
>
> They warned the Jewish people not to rely on blood offerings. Other methods of atonement were more efficacious and would even replace animal sacrifices. For example, King David cries out to God:
>
> > "Rescue me from bloodguilt, O G-d, G-d of my salvation. My L-rd, open my lips, that my mouth may declare Your praise. For You desire no offering, else I would give it, a burnt offering You do not favor. The offerings of G-d are a broken spirit, a heart broken and crushed O G-d, that You will not despise."
> > (Psalm 51:16-19 (14-17))[81]

The context of this psalm is David's adulterous act with Bathsheba followed by his attempt to cover it up by having her

---

[81] Rabbi Tovia Singer, *Let's Get Biblical* New Expanded Edition (Forest Hills, NY: Outreach Judaism, 2014), 2:307. In the Christian Bible, this is Psalm 51:14-17

husband, Uriah, murdered. David was wracked with guilt, and he thew himself on G-d's mercy. This is the correct response when we sin, to turn to G-d for mercy. David had a repentant heart. He hurt others, and he even killed an innocent man. After a while, he reached a point where he could clearly see how wrong he was, and given another chance, he would not have repeated those sins again. But in life we do not get another chance to do it all over again. G-d is merciful, but there must be justice. Someone must pay. That is why atonement is necessary, and David is not negating that in this psalm. Having a repentant heart does not, in and of itself, pay for your sins; it merely enables you to receive atonement.

Why did David write: "For you desire no offering, else I would give it, a burnt offering you do not favor."? It was not because G-d was waiving justice simply because David felt bad and he was asking for mercy. Perhaps David was expressing how completely inadequate the death of an unknowing animal would have been to pay the price for his grievous sins. Or perhaps he was trying to emphasize that what is important is to approach G-d with a broken and humble heart in order to receive forgiveness. Either way, he was not making a theological statement that G-d was willing to waive justice or that the Day of Atonement had become irrelevant. His point in this psalm is how amazing G-d's lovingkindness is. G-d is a G-d of "salvation." He will forgive even the most awful things we have done if only we will turn to Him for mercy.

9

A; B; C; D; __

The answer is E. It is not a trick question. It is a straightforward sequence.

The stories of Abraham and Isaac and the first Passover, along with G-d's design of the Tabernacle and His prescription of the rituals on the Day of Atonement, have much in common. They each:

1. are rich with symbolism pointing to something coming in the future;
2. are solemn, tragic, or terrifying as life and death hang in the balance;
3. are incongruous or incomplete to get your attention;
4. are fundamentally about the same subject, substitutionary atonement;
5. are events in which G-d provided for the deliverance of the Jews.

Now let's lay out these four passages in sequence and see how the pieces fit together to form a complete picture or message.

Abraham and Isaac: Abraham was called on to sacrifice his beloved son, Isaac, which made no sense because G-d is good. Furthermore, G-d had promised Abraham and Sarah a baby for many years; and their baby, Isaac, had a role to play which included having children before he died.

Thus, Abraham was shocked and confused when G-d called on him to take Isaac's life. But Abraham had learned to trust G-d, so he set out to carry out G-d's order. In the end, G-d provided a ram as a substitute, and Abraham was overjoyed.

G-d spoke to Abraham following the event and He praised Abraham for his faith. G-d also reiterated the covenant promises He had made previously to Abraham. But He did not explain why He had called on Abraham to sacrifice Isaac. Yet certainly, the fact that G-d called on Abraham to sacrifice Isaac was symbolic of a similar event that would take place in the future.

The Passover: On the night of the first Passover, G-d called on the Jews to sacrifice an unblemished lamb or goat in order to be spared from judgement consisting of the death of each family's firstborn son. Each family was to perform the sacrifice and put some of the blood on the sides and top of the doorframe around their front door. They obeyed, and G-d passed over every house with blood on the doorframe. However, in each Egyptian house, tragedy struck as the L-rd struck down the firstborn son of the household as well as the firstborn of their cattle. Every year since that first night, the Jews have gone on to perform rituals on Passover to celebrate their deliverance from both their Egyptian captors and G-d's judgement for their sins.

It is interesting that Moses directed the Jews to select the sacrificial lambs four days prior to slaying them. Surely G-d wanted the Jews to take a moment and think about how an innocent being was going to give up its life for them. It must have been a very solemn moment when the lambs were slain.

It is also interesting that on Passover, sacrificial lambs and goats stood in as substitutes in place of the firstborn sons, as that is exactly what happened with Abraham and Isaac. It appears to be a pattern.

The Tabernacle: The Tabernacle was also named the tent of meeting. This was the place where G-d dwelt in the midst of the Jewish people. The problem was, they could not actually meet with Him for they were unworthy to come into His presence. Hence, there was a veil to the inner sanctuary, the Holy of Holies, through which they could not enter, lest they die.

Have you ever seen a handicapped child sitting in a wheelchair? Maybe they are hunched over, or their hands and wrists are cocked at strange angles. It is so tragic. You think, "that poor child," and you know it is not supposed to be that way. So too, if you gazed upon the tent of meeting, you would have known that something was wrong as the quality of personal relating between G-d and His people was severely handicapped. For, the way the Jews related to G-d in the tent of meeting was through rituals. The predominant ritual was animal sacrifice. The Jewish historian, Josephus, recorded that one year during the reign of Nero, the priests kept track of the number of sacrificial lambs they offered at Passover, and it was 256,500.[82] Killing animals for sacrifices was a seven-day-a-week operation. It was factory-like, and it never stopped. But it is not supposed to be that way. G-d created us to personally know Him, not to kill animals on behalf of our sins.

The most important of the six pieces of furniture in the Tabernacle was the Ark of the Covenant in the Holy of Holies. It was essentially a box that contained evidence from three historic instances of Jewish sin and rebellion against G-d. The scene in the Holy of Holies was that of a courtroom in which the evidence proved the guilt of the Jewish people. The sentence for sin is death. However, the Ark of the Covenant had a very unusual lid. It was a mercy seat upon which the blood of an innocent substitute could be splattered to pay the price of justice for the sins of the Jewish people.

Yet, the Jewish people were strictly forbidden from going into the Holy of Holies to be in G-d's presence. This implies that the rituals of the Tabernacle were merely symbolic as they did not provide literal absolution of the Jews' sins. But surely, the elaborate symbology of the Tabernacle was pointing to something very important that would happen in the future in which the sins of the Jews would actually be paid for.

The Day of Atonement: As the Jews were in transit to the Promised Land, G-d gave specific instructions for performing

---

[82] Josephus Flavius, *The Wars of the Jews*, 6.9.3 (422-424) from: *The Works of Josephus*, Complete and Unabridged, New Updated Edition, trans. William Whiston, A.M. (Peabody, MA: Hendrickson Publishers, Inc., 2009) 749. [This reference of book 6, chapter 9, paragraph 3 (numbers 422 through 424) is per the Whiston numbering system in which the numbers given in parentheses correspond to the ones used in the Greek text.] (Alfred Edersheim, *The Temple: Its Ministry and Services*, updated ed. (Peabody, Massachusetts: Hendrickson Publishers, Inc., 1994) 168.)

ritual sacrifices and the special rituals that were to be observed on the Day of Atonement. Only on the Day of Atonement could the High Priest enter through the veil into the very presence of G-d in the Holy of Holies. There, he splattered the blood of a bull on the mercy seat for his own personal sins and the blood of a goat for the unintentional sins of the nation. Once he emerged from the presence of G-d, he placed his hands upon the head of the other goat and sent it away to carry the sins of the people deep into the wilderness. The Day of Atonement was held annually, and the people were responsible to be there. Further, they were to contemplate their moral failures and be humble. Also, the day was to be an extra Sabbath and no work was permitted. They were to know that there were no works they could perform to earn right standing before G-d. They were in need of a substitute, and all they could do was hold up empty hands of faith and receive atonement as a gift from G-d.

The answer is Jesus. He is the fulfillment of this sequence of passages dealing with sacrifices in the Torah.

Jesus' Crucifixion: It says in Genesis 22:3 that prior to setting out on the three-day journey, "Abraham rose early in the morning and saddled his donkey." Certainly, for at least part of the journey, Abraham had his beloved son sit upon the donkey. Approximately two thousand years later, another descendant of Abraham would be seated on a donkey as He approached Jerusalem. His name was Jesus; and like Isaac, His conception was miraculous too.

A few days after Jesus arrived in Jerusalem, on the eve of His sacrificial death, He was deep in thought, just as Abraham must have been throughout his three-day journey to Mt.

Moriah. Jesus knew what lay ahead of Him and that it would be horrendous. It was the middle of the night, and He was in a garden praying to G-d. He was very upset, and He asked G-d: "My Father, if it is possible, let this cup pass from Me; yet not as I will, but as Thou wilt."[83] Unlike the case of Isaac, G-d did not provide a way out for Jesus. It was not possible. It was necessary for a real substitute to step in and pay the price of justice for the sins of humanity. For without a substitute, we must pay the price ourselves; and that price is eternal separation from G-d. Jesus either heard from G-d the answer 'no', or He understood the answer to be no from G-d's silence. The passage does not tell us which one it was. But surely Jesus knew the answer. For, immediately after praying, He rose to go and meet His betrayer, Judas, and the armed band of men Judas brought to arrest Him.[84] Jesus' trial and execution followed shortly thereafter.

Interestingly, just as Isaac carried the bundle of wood for the fire two thousand years earlier, so too, prior to collapsing, Jesus carried the wooden cross on His back as they proceeded to the spot where He was to be crucified. Then, in a move only G-d could make, Jesus perished on a Roman cross in the same location where Abraham was to offer Isaac as a burnt offering.[85] In so doing, Jesus fulfilled what was foreshadowed by G-d two thousand years earlier when He called for Isaac to be offered as a sacrifice.

A few years earlier, John the Baptist had called Jesus "the Lamb of G-d." Sure enough, Jesus was crucified during the Passover Week. Similar to the Passover lamb, which was physically unblemished, Jesus was sinless and morally unblemished.

---

[83] Mt. 26:39.
[84] Mk. 14:43.
[85] 2 Chron. 3:1.

Much like the blood of the Passover lambs that was painted on the doorframes of the Jewish homes, Jesus' blood flowed from the wounds in His hands and feet onto the vertical and horizontal wooden beams of His cross.

On Passover, the slain lambs were roasted in fire without any of their bones being broken.[86] Jesus perished on the cross before the two criminals who were crucified alongside Him. As it was starting to get late in the day and the Sabbath was approaching, the Jews asked Pilate to have the soldiers break the legs of those being crucified because they needed to take the bodies down so they did not violate the Mosaic Law. This was common practice as breaking a crucifixion victim's legs prevented him from being able to lift himself to breathe, thereby hastening his death. But when the soldiers came to Jesus, He was already dead, so they abstained.[87] Hence, just like all of the Passover lambs dating all the way back to the very first Passover, Jesus' bones remained unbroken.

Whereas sacrificial animals were slain as humanely as possible, it is hard to conceive of a scenario that would be more inhumane than the way Jesus' murder unfolded. Jesus was punched in the face, whipped to the point that His back was ripped open, stripped of His clothes, spit on, mocked, and nailed to a cross until He died. In so doing, He bore the wrath of G-d in our place. Unlike the Day of Atonement, where the sacrifices had to be repeated yearly, Jesus' death on the cross will never have to be repeated again.

In the Christian New Testament, the book of Hebrews is a letter written specifically to Jews explaining the Day of Atonement in light of Jesus' crucifixion. The message of Hebrews is that all of the symbology from the Day of Atonement pointed to Jesus dying on the cross. Following His

---

[86] Ex. 12:46.

[87] Jn. 19:31-37.

crucifixion, in correlation to the High Priest sprinkling the mercy seat with blood, Jesus would go on to present His blood to G-d; and it actually covers the cost of the sins of humanity.[88] Jesus is the G-d-sized solution pictured by all of the symbols of the Day of Atonement.

Jesus' love is amazing. He did not have to go through with it. But for our sakes, He did. While Jesus was on the cross dying, one of the criminals being crucified next to Him reached out to Him for help. Jesus said to him, ". . . today you shall be with Me in paradise."[89] For this purpose Jesus came, to save sinners, including both Jews and Gentiles.[90]

It says in The Gospel According to Matthew that when Jesus breathed His last, the veil to the Holy of Holies in the Temple tore in half from top to bottom.[91] The message of the Christian New Testament is that through Jesus' sacrifice, we can now come into G-d's presence.[92] We can commune with Jesus in this life as He will come into our hearts if we say yes to Him; and we will see G-d face-to-face in the next life.[93] In the words of Jesus: "Behold, I stand at the door and knock; if anyone hears My voice and opens the door, I will come in to him, and dine with him, and he with Me."[94]

In The Gospel According to John, John wrote that Jesus came to His own people, and they rejected Him.[95] Not all, but as a whole, the Jews rejected Jesus. That was not what Jesus wanted, but it was what they chose. So too, each individual

---

[88] Heb. 9:11-15, 24; 10:1-23.

[89] Lk. 23:43.

[90] Jn. 12:27.

[91] Mt. 27:50-51.

[92] Heb. 10:19-22.

[93] 1 Cor. 13:12.

[94] Rev. 3:20.

[95] Jn. 1:11.

today must choose to accept or reject G-d's free offer of atonement through Jesus.[96]

There are no words to describe how great a sacrifice Jesus made on behalf of mankind. Please don't take it lightly. Be careful not to listen to pat answers by people who pull a handful of statements out of the Hebrew Bible in an attempt to disprove that Jesus is the savior of mankind. Read the Bible for yourself. It is easy for people to confidently direct you here on earth, but they will not be standing next to you when you are standing before G-d. Pray to G-d. Ask Him to show you what His selection of Isaac to be a burnt offering was foreshadowing and what all of the symbols from Passover, the Tabernacle, and the Day of Atonement represent. He put a lot of effort into that symbology. I believe He wants the sincere of heart to know what it means.

* * * * *

But what about the parts of Jesus' story that do not line up with these passages from the Torah, you may ask? I do not believe there are any such parts.

---

[96] Jn. 1:12; 14:6.

Below is a list of all the relevant passages if you would like to read them for yourself.

Abraham and Isaac:	Gen. 22:1-19
The Passover:	Ex. 11:1-13:16
The Tabernacle:	Ex. 25:1-31:11; 35:4-40:38
The Day of Atonement:	Lev. 16-17; 23:26-32; Num. 29:7-11
Jesus' Crucifixion:	Mt. 26:30-27:66; Mk. 14:26-15:47; Lk. 22:39-23:56; Jn. 18:1-19:42

part three

TYPES

10

JOSEPH'S HEART OF FORGIVENESS

In chapter 4 of this book, we defined types as follows:

> Types are real people whose lives in some way
> foreshadow the actions, experiences, or role
> of another person who has been prophesied
> to one day come and play a part in G-d's plan.
> Hence, when the future person comes along
> and takes their place on the stage of history,
> we can identify them as we observe the
> connection between their life and that of the
> earlier person.

Now let's look at some specific examples of types. In all of
the examples, we will compare the lives of people from the
Hebrew Bible with the life of Jesus. The question is whether

Christians are reading too much into the lives of these heroes from the Hebrew Bible, or whether there is something there.

We will begin with Joseph, who played a major part in the book of Genesis. Of course, the three patriarchs are Abraham, Isaac, and Jacob. Yet, much is written about Joseph as well. Of the fifty chapters in Genesis, Abraham is the main subject in twelve of them,[97] Isaac is the main subject in three,[98] and Jacob is the main subject in twelve.[99] But there are ten chapters in which Joseph is the main subject.[100]

Of the ten chapters about Joseph, eight of them are about the defining moment in his life; namely, when he was betrayed by his older brothers. Chapter 37 tells the story of the betrayal, chapters 38 through 40 cover the suffering that ensued in Joseph's life, and chapters 42 through 45 cover Joseph's forgiveness of his brothers and his reconciliation with them many years later.

In Genesis chapter 5, whole generations are covered in a few sentences each. But when we come to the four-chapter span starting with chapter 42, the pace of the writing is considerably slower as the story of Joseph reconciling with his brothers is depicted in fine detail. There is something very important that G-d wants us to learn about Joseph's forgiveness and efforts to reconcile with his brothers.

It all started when Jacob was tricked by his father-in-law, Laban, and spent his wedding night with Leah, rather than his beloved fiancée, Rachel.[101] Ironically, Jacob was defrauded by the same scam he perpetrated to cheat his brother out of their father's blessing.[102] In the dark, on the wedding night, Leah

---

[97] Gen. 12-23.
[98] Gen. 24-26.
[99] Gen. 27-35; 46; 48-49.
[100] Gen. 37; 39-45; 47; 50.
[101] Gen. 29:23.
[102] Gen. 27.

was the one who came into the bridal chamber. Perhaps Jacob had some wine during the feast, for the ruse worked. But when morning came, Jacob discovered what happened, and he was not happy. However, he was able to marry Rachel after working another seven years for Laban as a shepherd. As the years went by, he had ten sons and a daughter with Leah and his two concubines, but none with Rachel. Finally, Rachel bore a son, Joseph. By this point, Jacob was getting old, and Joseph was his favorite. Needless to say, Joseph's brothers were jealous.

As a teenager, Joseph had a pair of dreams in which his parents and brothers bowed down to him. He told them about his dreams, and his brothers' resentment grew into loathing.[103] When Jacob sent Joseph to check on his brothers as they were shepherding in Shechem, they saw him coming over the rise. Their ill will bubbled over into violence, and they ripped his robe off of him and threw him in a pit. Then a caravan of Midianite traders passed by, and Joseph's brothers sold him to them for twenty shekels of silver.[104] From there, the Midianites took him to Egypt where he was sold as a slave.[105] Meanwhile, the brothers dipped his robe in blood, and brought it back to Jacob stating that they found it and thought it might be Joseph's. It was a unique robe, and Jacob knew it was Joseph's. Jacob was heartbroken for he believed that Joseph had been eaten by a wild beast.

Joseph suffered for many years in Egypt, first as a slave, and then as a prisoner when his master's wife falsely accused him of attempted rape. Through it all, G-d was with him. G-d blessed every effort of his hands, and Joseph was well liked by all who came in contact with him.

---

[103] Gen. 37:5-11.
[104] Gen. 37:28.
[105] Gen. 37:36.

Joseph was not like his brothers. He was godly. He did not go down their path of harboring ill will towards them for what they had done. He understood that life is about more than our circumstances. Life is about following the will of G-d. Furthermore, not only was G-d with him each day as he went through the prime of his life without freedom, but also G-d had given him a pair of prophetic dreams as a youth. In his dreams, G-d revealed to him that one day, G-d would elevate him to a high position in which his brothers and even his father and mother would bow down to him.[106]

While Joseph was languishing in the Egyptian jail, the pharaoh became angry with his cupbearer and his chief baker, and they were thrown into jail alongside Joseph.[107] These two both had vivid dreams one night, and they knew there was something unusual about their dreams. They were right. Their dreams were prophetic. Fortunately for them, Joseph received from G-d the interpretation of their dreams. Joseph revealed to the cupbearer good news that within three days he would be released from prison and restored to his office. But the interpretation for the chief baker was not good. Joseph told him that in three days Pharaoh will "hang you on a tree; and the birds will eat your flesh."[108] Sure enough, both interpretations came true just as Joseph predicted.

Joseph asked the cupbearer to put in a good word for him with Pharaoh to see if perhaps he could be set free. But the cupbearer forgot. However, two years later, Pharaoh had a couple disturbing dreams of his own. Then the cupbearer remembered, and he told Pharaoh about Joseph. Joseph was called, and again G-d gave him the interpretation of the dreams. It involved a seven-year-long famine that would come

---

[106] Gen. 37:10.
[107] Gen. 40:3.
[108] Gen. 40:19.

following seven years of good harvests. The pharaoh knew in his heart that Joseph was right. Joseph also gave some suggestions as to how to go about saving the excess grain from the bountiful years in preparation for the very difficult years to follow. Pharaoh was so impressed that he put Joseph in charge of the effort. In fact, he elevated Joseph to the second highest position in all of Egypt, just below himself![109]

Thus, in the blink of an eye, Joseph's circumstances went from as bad as they could be to the exact opposite. He was thirty years old at this time.[110] In all, he was oppressed for thirteen years. That is the length of time that his brothers stole from him.

Several years later, when the famine came, Joseph's family was starving in Canaan. But they heard about the availability of food in Egypt. So the ten older brothers came to Egypt to acquire some provisions. Lo and behold, who did they come face to face with? Of course, Joseph. But they did not recognize him as the last time they saw him he was seventeen, and now he was around forty. Also, he was speaking Egyptian and he was dressed like a wealthy Egyptian. But he recognized them:

> . . . And Joseph remembered the dreams which he had about them, and said to them, "You are spies; you have come to look at the undefended parts of our land." Then they said to him, "No, my lord, but your servants have come to buy food. We are all sons of one man; we are honest men, your servants are not spies." Yet he said to them, "No, but you have come to look at the undefended parts of our

---

[109] Gen. 41:40-45.
[110] Gen. 41:46.

land!" But they said, "Your servants are twelve brothers *in all*, the sons of one man in the land of Canaan; and behold, the youngest is with our father today, and one is no more." And Joseph said to them, "It is as I said to you, you are spies; by this you will be tested: by the life of Pharaoh, you shall not go from this place unless your youngest brother comes here! Send one of you that he may get your brother, while you remain confined, that your words may be tested, whether there is truth in you. But if not, by the life of Pharaoh, surely you are spies." So he put them all together in prison for three days.

Now Joseph said to them on the third day, "Do this and live, for I fear G-d: if you are honest men, let one of your brothers be confined in your prison; but as for *the rest of* you, go, carry grain for the famine of your households, and bring your youngest brother to me, so your words may be verified, and you will not die." And they did so. Then they said to one another, "Truly we are guilty concerning our brother, because we saw the distress of his soul when he pleaded with us, yet we would not listen; therefore this distress has come upon us." And Reuben answered them, saying, "Did I not tell you, 'Do not sin against the boy'; and you would not listen? Now comes the reckoning for his blood." They did not know, however, that Joseph understood, for there was an interpreter between them. And he turned away from them and wept. But when he returned to them and spoke to them, he took Simeon from them and bound him before their eyes.

Then Joseph gave orders to fill their bags with grain and to restore every man's money in his sack, and to give them provisions for the journey. And thus it was done for them.[111]

So Joseph put his brothers under pressure. In the midst of the confrontation, he heard them speak about him and it moved him to tears. He learned that they regretted what they had done. But was it because of the pain they caused him, or because of the consequences they were facing? In addition, he found out that his oldest brother, Reuben, had stood up for him. That must have been heartening. His tears were tears of warmth. Yet he was not going to let them off easy. Therefore, he threw Simeon in jail while releasing the others to go and bring back the youngest brother he just found out about. But his motives were not to make them pay, for he had already forgiven them. Rather, he was being hard on them in order to resolve the conflict more deeply for their sakes.

So the brothers returned home without Simeon. They told their father about their dealings with this harsh Egyptian ruler, and how he wanted them to return with their youngest brother, Benjamin. But in no way was Jacob willing to risk losing his only remaining son from his wife, Rachel, by sending him on this journey. However, as the days wore on and the famine persisted, they came under increasing pressure to return to Egypt because they were starving. So, Judah swore to his father that he would be responsible for

---

[111] Gen. 42:9-25.

Benjamin's safe return; and Jacob relented and let them take Benjamin.[112]

When they arrived, of all things, Joseph had them come to his home for a meal. When Joseph saw his younger brother Benjamin for the first time, he was filled with emotion. In fact, he had to leave the room to weep; for he did not want them to see him crying as he was continuing the ruse. He was still not done testing them. Here is what happened when he later sent all eleven brothers back to Canaan with their packs filled with grain:

> Then he commanded his house steward, saying, "Fill the men's sacks with food, as much as they can carry, and put each man's money in the mouth of his sack. And put my cup, the silver cup, in the mouth of the sack of the youngest, and his money for the grain." And he did as Joseph had told *him*. As soon as it was light, the men were sent away, they with their donkeys. They had *just* gone out of the city, *and* were not far off, when Joseph said to his house steward, "Up, follow the men; and when you overtake them, say to them, 'Why have you repaid evil for good? Is not this the one from which my lord drinks, and which he indeed uses for divination? You have done wrong in doing this.'"[113]

So the house steward caught up to Joseph's brothers and accused them of stealing. They vehemently denied it. But, to their shock, when their sacks were opened, Joseph's cup was

---

[112] Gen. 43:8-13.
[113] Gen. 44:1-5.

in Benjamin's sack. Then they were led back to the city to face Joseph:

> When Judah and his brothers came to Joseph's house, he was still there, and they fell to the ground before him. And Joseph said to them, "What is this deed that you have done? Do you not know that such a man as I can indeed practice divination?" So Judah said, "What can we say to my lord? What can we speak? And how can we justify ourselves? G-d has found out the iniquity of your servants; behold we are my lord's slaves, both we and the one in whose possession the cup has been found." But he said, "Far be it from me to do this. The man in whose possession the cup has been found, he shall be my slave; but as for you, go up in peace to your father."
>
> Then Judah approached him, and said, "Oh my lord, may your servant please speak a word in my lord's ears, and do not be angry with your servant; for you are equal to Pharaoh. My lord asked his servants, saying, 'Have you a father or a brother?' And we said to my lord, 'We have an old father and a little child of *his* old age. Now his brother is dead, so he alone is left of his mother, and his father loves him.' . . . Now, therefore, when I come to your servant my father, and the lad is not *with us*, since his life is bound up in the lad's life, it will come about when he sees that the lad is not with us, that he will die. Thus your servants will bring the gray hair of your servant our father down to Sheol in sorrow.

For your servant became surety for the lad to my father, saying, 'If I do not bring him *back* to you, then let me bear the blame before my father forever.' Now, therefore, please let your servant remain instead of the lad a slave to my lord, and let the lad go up with his brothers. For how shall I go up to my father if the lad is not with me, lest I see the evil that would overtake my father?"

Then Joseph could not control himself before all those who stood by him, and he cried, "Have everyone go out from me." So there was no man with him when Joseph made himself known to his brothers. And he wept so loudly that the Egyptians heard it, and the household of Pharaoh heard *of it*. Then Joseph said to his brothers, "I am Joseph! Is my father still alive?" But his brothers could not answer him, for they were dismayed at his presence. Then Joseph said to his brothers, "Please come closer to me." And they came closer. And he said, "I am your brother Joseph, whom you sold into Egypt. And now do not be grieved or angry with yourselves, because you sold me here; for G-d sent me before you to preserve life. . . ." . . . And he kissed all his brothers and wept on them, and afterward his brothers talked with him.[114]

Joseph put them under pressure again! This time, Judah spoke up and pleaded for Joseph to take him as a slave and let

---

[114] Gen. 44:14-20, 30-34; 45:1-5, 15.

Benjamin go free for the sake of their father, Jacob. This is what Joseph was looking for. Judah and his brothers had learned their lesson. Judah now cared more about the wellbeing of others than he cared about himself. Immediately Joseph ended the ruse. He revealed himself and received his brothers in love.

In what way is this detailed account of forgiveness and reconciliation typical of Jesus' story? In every way. The essence of Jesus' mission was to provide forgiveness for sins. In the words of Jesus as the Roman soldiers were crucifying Him: "Father, forgive them; for they do not know what they are doing."[115] The forgiveness offered by Jesus on the basis of His sacrificial death is the bridge by which we can be reconciled to G-d:

> . . . Now all *these* things are from G-d, who reconciled us to Himself through Christ, and gave us the ministry of reconciliation, namely, that G-d was in Christ reconciling the world to Himself, not counting their trespasses against them, and He has committed to us the word of reconciliation. Therefore, we are ambassadors for Christ, as though G-d were entreating through us; we beg you on behalf of Christ, be reconciled to G-d. He made Him who knew no sin *to be* sin on our behalf, that we might become the righteousness of G-d in Him.[116]

This reconciliation encompasses peace with G-d in this life and the next. In this life, G-d pours His love into your heart

---

[115] Lk. 23:34.
[116] 2 Cor. 5:18-21.

to heal you and transform you into a conduit for His love to flow to others. In the words of Jesus: "Behold, I stand at the door and knock; if anyone hears My voice and opens the door, I will come in to him, and will dine with him, and he with Me."[117] Certainly, this reconciliation is eternal as well, for Jesus' sacrificial death is the way G-d provided for us to be forgiven and enter His presence in heaven.[118] There, we will have a relationship with Him in the way that Adam and Eve once did.

Of course, Jesus paid a high price to provide this forgiveness. In Philippians 2:8, it says: "And being found in appearance as a man, He humbled Himself by becoming obedient to the point of death, even death on a cross." His death was awful. The Romans were very good at some things. For example, they were very good at fighting wars and building public works projects. Ironically, their army was equally adept at destroying things. Another area in which they were brilliant was executing people. The Romans used public crucifixion to terrify the people they conquered so that they would not rebel. In crucifixion, death came by torture. It was an extremely painful way to die, and it took multiple hours, if not days, for the poor soul to pass away. Somehow, to pay the price for the sins of humanity, it required Jesus to be crucified; to which He said, let it be so! While on the cross, He bore the wrath of G-d. Of course, it is not possible for a single human being to bear the wrath of G-d for the sins of all people of all time. That is why Jesus had to come down from heaven and take on the form of a man. He could do it. While on the cross, Jesus said, "Eli, Eli, lama sabachthani?", that is, "My G-d, My

---

[117] Rev. 3:20.
[118] Jn. 3:16-18; 14:6.

G-d, Why hast Thou forsaken Me?"[119] It had to be so in order for the price of our sins to be covered.

Joseph had prepared his brothers to be reconciled with him. That is what the events in Genesis chapters 42 through 45 are all about. While in Egypt, Joseph did not know what became of his brothers. After all, anger begets anger. Did they go down a path of crime after accosting him and selling him into slavery? Or did they turn from their sinful ways? He had no way of knowing.

His brothers were able to come to Egypt when they needed to buy food to save their lives. But, in all the years prior to that, they had never come to redeem his life. At their first encounter, they told him they were "honest men,"[120] but they were not; for they were still maintaining their lie about Joseph to their father.[121] Thus, Joseph continued his ruse to see if these men had learned their lesson and could be trusted. Indeed, he even needed to find out if they still loathed him or not, for reconciliation requires the willing participation of both parties.

Fortunately, it ended well for Joseph and his family. His brothers responded humbly, and the result was healing and unity. In addition, Joseph had the entire Jewish clan move from Canaan to Egypt where they were spared from the famine. Unfortunately, over time they became enslaved in Egypt until G-d sent Moses to deliver them 430 years later.[122]

So too, Jesus spent approximately three-and-a-half years preparing the nation to be reconciled with G-d. He healed those with diseases and birth defects, received the lowly with grace and kindness, performed various other breathtaking

---

[119] Mt. 27:46.
[120] Gen. 42:11.
[121] Gen. 42:38.
[122] Ex. 12:41.

miracles, prophesied, raised up a band of disciples, fulfilled a large portion of the messianic prophecy in the Hebrew Bible, clashed with people who were illicitly profiting in the Temple grounds, debated with the Pharisees, and preached a message of forgiveness for sins. His desire was for the Jewish people to embrace His message and personally find G-d;[123] but sadly, He was largely rejected by the Jewish people.

* * * * *

There are also other details of Joseph's story in which there are parallels between his life and Jesus' life. These parallel details appear to have been recorded to show us that Joseph is a type of Jesus. One of these details is that they were both unceremoniously disrobed. Joseph was disrobed by his brothers and thrown in a pit. They hated his special, multicolored robe that their father had given him,[124] and they proceeded to dip it in blood as a prop supporting their lie. In Jesus' case, the Roman soldiers took His robe off and then famously gambled for it as if it were a souvenir.[125]

Another detail in which there is a parallel between what happened to Joseph and what happened to Jesus has to do with Joseph's two fellow prisoners. Joseph proclaimed to one of them that he would be set free, and to the other that he would be executed; and so they were. In Jesus' case, two criminals were crucified next to Him, one on His right and one on His left. One of them turned to Him for mercy and received salvation. The other one joined in with the crowd mocking Him. That man received judgement in this life, and sadly, he will in the next as well.[126]

---

[123] Mt. 23:37.
[124] Gen. 37:3.
[125] Mt. 27:35.
[126] Lk. 23:39-43.

Both Joseph and Jesus were betrayed and sold for filthy lucre: Joseph for twenty pieces of silver,[127] and Jesus for thirty.[128]

Thus, there are conspicuous parallels between Joseph's life and Jesus' life. But the main one has to do with Joseph's forgiveness towards his brothers, including the effort he made to be reconciled with them. G-d emphasizes this part of Joseph's life story in the book of Genesis as He devotes four chapters to it. Of course, that is because we need to learn to forgive people in order to experience happiness and healthy relationships in life. But even more important than that, we each need to receive G-d's forgiveness for our wrongdoings and be reconciled with Him in order to be whole in this life and for the sake of our eternal destinies. That is why Jesus came two thousand years ago—to provide atonement for our sins and to extend an offer of reconciliation to us.

What a truly good, godly man Joseph was. Joseph's heart of forgiveness is a picture of Jesus' heart.

---

[127] Gen. 37:28.
[128] Mt. 26:15.

11

MOSES THE MEDIATOR

Moses was a humble man.[129] Paradoxically, he was a great leader. But in a way, that makes sense, because someone who knows who they are and who submits themself to G-d's will for their life will be used by G-d to do great things.

A good example of Moses' humility is the story in Numbers chapter 11 where the Holy Spirit used two Jewish men in the camp to prophesy. Moses was not upset that G-d had chosen others in addition to him to speak on His behalf; rather, he embraced it. Thus, Moses stood in stark contrast to typical human kings, who, at the faintest whiff of a potential rival, act to eliminate them.

---

[129] Num. 12:3.

So too, Jesus was not arrogant. He loved all people from His heart, including the lowly. For example, here is how Jesus treated a man with leprosy:

> And a leper came to Him, beseeching Him and falling on his knees before Him, and saying to Him, "If You are willing, You can make me clean." And moved with compassion, He stretched out His hand, and touched him, and said to him, "I am willing; be cleansed." And immediately the leprosy left him and he was cleansed.[130]

In the ancient world, leprosy was a curse. It was disfiguring, disabling, and humiliating, and eventually, it killed you. But if that was not enough, you were not permitted to live with everyone else. People were scared to touch you. If anyone came near you, you had to yell out, "Unclean! Unclean!"[131] Therefore, not only did this disease rob you of your physical health, but it also took your dignity and sense of self-worth.

In the case of this poor soul, he approached Jesus and timidly asked Him for a miracle. Jesus was "moved with compassion" by this man's plight. Then Jesus did the unthinkable; He touched him and showed him kindness and acceptance. Needless to say, Jesus also healed him and gave him his life back. This is the way Jesus acted when He was amongst us. He did not seek recognition from people in high positions. Rather, He cared deeply for the lowly and the hurting.

---

[130] Mk. 1:40-42.
[131] Lev. 13:45-46.

Neither Moses nor Jesus cared about their own personal glory, but rather, they cared only about the will of G-d and people. This heart attitude enabled Moses to not only be a great leader, but also to be a mediator between G-d and man.

In Exodus 32, as Moses was speaking with G-d on the mountain and the Jews were committing their epic act of betrayal down below, the Hebrew Bible says:

> ... Then the L-rd spoke to Moses, "Go down at once, for your people, whom you brought up from the land of Egypt, have corrupted *themselves*. They have quickly turned aside from the way which I commanded them. They have made for themselves a molten calf, and have worshiped it, and have sacrificed to it, and said, 'This is your god, O Israel, who brought you up from the land of Egypt!'" And the L-rd said to Moses, "I have seen this people, and behold, they are an obstinate people. Now then let Me alone, that My anger may burn against them, and that I may destroy them; and I will make of you a great nation."

> Then Moses entreated the L-rd his G-d, and said, "O, L-rd, why doth Thine anger burn against Thy people whom Thou hast brought out from the land of Egypt with great power and with a mighty hand? Why should the Egyptians speak, saying, 'With evil *intent* He brought them out to kill them in the mountains and to destroy them from the face of the earth'? Turn from Thy burning anger and change Thy mind about *doing* harm to Thy people. Remember Abraham, Isaac, and

Israel, Thy servants to whom Thou didst swear by Thyself, and didst say to them, 'I will multiply your descendants as the stars of the heavens, and all this land of which I have spoken I will give to your descendants, and they shall inherit *it* forever.'" So the L-rd changed His mind about the harm which He said He would do to His people.[132]

In this passage, Moses intervened on behalf of the Jewish people. G-d offered to start over with Moses, but that did not appeal to Moses. Instead, he pled with G-d to let the Jews go free. It is notable that he did not argue for the Jews to be given another chance based on their worthiness. Rather, his argument had to do with G-d's reputation among the nations and G-d's faithfulness to the promises He made to Abraham, Isaac, and Jacob. No doubt, G-d was pleased with Moses and the case he made, as He rescinded His statement regarding the destruction of the entire nation except for Moses.

When Moses went down the mountain, he beheld the Jewish people in spiritual and moral free fall, and it was disgusting. Now he saw what G-d was seeing. Now he understood the nature and the gravity of their rebellion; and now he became angry, too. Moses did his best to clean up the mess, and then he went back up the mountain. Even though G-d had already relented from His threat to execute judgement on the nation, Moses felt the need to plead again for their forgiveness:

... "Alas, this people has committed a great sin, and they have made a god of gold for themselves. But now, if Thou wilt, forgive their sin—and if not, please blot me out from

---

[132] Ex. 32:7-14.

Thy book which Thou hast written!" And the
L-rd said to Moses, "Whoever has sinned
against Me, I will blot him out of My book.
But go now, lead the people where I told you.
Behold, My angel shall go before you;
nevertheless in the day when I punish, I will
punish them for their sin." Then the L-rd
smote the people, because of what they did
with the calf which Aaron had made.[133]

Moses witnessed the Jews' great sin, and he
acknowledged it to G-d. Nonetheless, Moses was so
committed to serving the Jewish people that he asked to be
blotted out from G-d's book if G-d would not spare this people.
This could mean either that he was asking to die or to be
destined for hell.

What a truly great leader Moses was. He cared for the
Jewish people from the bottom of his heart. He was so devoted
to them that he came to identify with them. Furthermore, he
may have felt responsible for their moral failure, because he
was their leader. Therefore, he made this bitter request to G-d.
But G-d is the one who understands justice with infallible
precision; and Moses was not responsible for the Jews' lack of
faith and betrayal of G-d. Thus, the L-rd smote some of the
Jews with a plague and they perished. But He allowed the rest
to go on living. In regard to Moses, G-d would hold him
accountable, but only for his own sins. Hence, although Moses
would live to be very old and lead the Jewish people all the
way to the precipice of entering the promised land, he would
not be allowed to enter it.[134] It would be then that Moses' days
on earth would come to an end. Albeit, G-d was very gracious

---

[133] Ex. 32:31-35.
[134] Deut. 32:48-52.

to Moses and was with him in a tangible way at the end of his life.[135]

Interestingly, a couple of years before this event on Mt. Sinai, Moses' self-confidence was broken. So, he argued with G-d to try to get out of having to deal with the Egyptian pharaoh on behalf of the Jews.[136] Now he is arguing with G-d again. Only, this time, he is arguing for the Jews to be set free from having to pay the price of justice for their sins. Now Moses' eyes are not on himself and his own limitations; now his eyes are on the plight of others. Moses had grown as a person. He grew in his love for the Jewish people, and he became brave.

Thus, G-d would permit the Jewish people to go on. But He was not pleased with them, and He would no longer travel with them.[137] Previously, G-d was with the Jews and led them by day as a pillar of cloud and by night as a pillar of fire.[138] Moses pushed back on G-d again. However, this time it was for himself as well as for the people, for Moses had a special relationship with G-d, and he did not want to lose that. As it says in Exodus 33:

> . . . And it came about, whenever Moses entered the tent, the pillar of cloud would descend and stand at the entrance of the tent; and the L-rd would speak with Moses. When all the people saw the pillar of cloud standing at the entrance of the tent, all the people would arise and worship, each at the entrance of his tent. Thus the L-rd used to speak to Moses face to face, just as a man speaks to his

---

[135] Deut 34:1-8.
[136] Ex. 3:11; 4:13.
[137] Ex. 33:5.
[138] Ex. 13:21.

friend. When Moses returned to the camp, his servant Joshua, the son of Nun, a young man, would not depart from the tent.

Then Moses said to the L-rd, "See, Thou dost say to me, 'Bring up this people!' But Thou Thyself hast not let me know whom Thou wilt send with me. Moreover, Thou hast said, 'I have known you by name, and you have also found favor in My sight.' Now therefore, I pray Thee, if I have found favor in Thy sight, let me know Thy ways, that I may know Thee, so that I may find favor in Thy sight. Consider too, that this nation is Thy people." And He said, "My presence shall go with you, and I will give you rest." Then he said to Him, "If Thy presence does not go *with* us, do not lead us up from here. For how then can it be known that I have found favor in Thy sight, I and Thy people? Is it not by Thy going with us, so that we, I and Thy people, may be distinguished from all the *other* people who are upon the face of the earth."

And the L-rd said to Moses, "I will also do this thing of which you have spoken; for you have found favor in My sight, and I have known you by name."[139]

G-d was very pleased with Moses, and He responded positively again to Moses' plea. This time He agreed to continue to be physically present with the Jews on their journey. In the next verse, Moses made another request:

---

[139] Ex. 33:9-17.

... Then Moses said, "I pray Thee, show me Thy glory!" And He said, "I myself will make all My goodness pass before you, and will proclaim the name of the L-rd before you; and I will be gracious to whom I will be gracious, and will show compassion on whom I will show compassion." But He said, "You cannot see My face, for no man can see Me and live!" Then the L-rd said, "Behold, there is a place by Me, and you shall stand *there* on the rock; and it will come about, while My glory is passing by, that I will put you in the cleft of the rock and cover you with My hand until I have passed by. Then I will take My hand away and you shall see My back, but My face shall not be seen."[140]

There was no end to what Moses was willing to ask G-d, and to what G-d was willing to grant. Here is what happened:

... And the L-rd descended in the cloud and stood there with him as he called upon the name of the L-rd. Then the L-rd passed by in front of him and proclaimed, "The L-rd, the L-rd G-d, compassionate and gracious, slow to anger, and abounding in lovingkindness and truth; who keeps lovingkindness for thousands, who forgives iniquity, transgression and sin; yet He will by no means leave *the guilty* unpunished, visiting the iniquity of fathers on the children and on the grandchildren to the third and fourth

---

[140] Ex. 33:18-23.

generations." And Moses made haste to bow
low toward the earth and worship.[141]

How fantastic! Moses had a visual encounter with G-d,
albeit limited by necessity. Moses' goal from the beginning
was to know G-d more deeply, and G-d obliged him by not
only showing Himself, but also by telling him about Himself.
First and foremost, He is a G-d of lovingkindness and
forgiveness. Yet, "He will by no means leave the guilty
unpunished."[142] What a paradox. G-d is a G-d who forgives
transgressions, and yet He will not compromise justice?
Clearly G-d spoke these words to get our attention and make
us think about how there must be something more to the
story.

The other lesson to be learned from Moses' requests is
that G-d was pleased when Moses asked to remain close to
Him and to get to know Him personally. In fact, G-d is pleased
when anyone makes a request like this. He will honor this
request from anyone, and it will be personal and life-giving.
Are you willing to draw close to G-d like this?

But there is still another miraculous detail to this story:

> And it came about when Moses was coming
> down from Mount Sinai (and the two tablets
> of the testimony were in Moses' hand as he
> was coming down from the mountain), that
> Moses did not know that the skin of his face
> shone because of his speaking with Him. So
> when Aaron and all the sons of Israel saw
> Moses, behold, the skin of his face shone, and
> they were afraid to come near him. Then

---

[141] Ex. 34:5-8.
[142] Ex. 34:7.

Moses called to them, and Aaron and all the rulers in the congregation returned to him; and Moses spoke to them. And afterward all the sons of Israel came near, and he commanded them *to do* everything that the L-rd had spoken to him on Mount Sinai. When Moses had finished speaking with them, he put a veil over his face. But whenever Moses went in before the L-rd to speak with Him, he would take off the veil until he came out; and whenever he came out and spoke to the sons of Israel what he had been commanded, the sons of Israel would see the face of Moses, that the skin of Moses' face shone. So Moses would replace the veil over his face until he went in to speak with Him.[143]

Was Moses' face radioactive? No, but it glowed. G-d can do that. For example, He created some fish that live in the deepest parts of the ocean to be iridescent and glow. Here He created an effect on Moses' face. In this way, the people got to see a glimpse of G-d like Moses did, only indirectly. Also, and more importantly, Moses' face was a strong reminder that Moses was imparting the very words of G-d, and the people needed to listen closely and obey.[144]

So how does this story foreshadow Jesus? The main parallel between Moses and Jesus is that they were both mediators between G-d and man. They were both brave, and they loved others more than even their own lives. Only, Jesus

---

[143] Ex.34:29-35.
[144] Deut. 18:15-19.

was an order of magnitude higher as a mediator.[145] For Jesus was not only a mediator or priest, but He was also the sacrifice! Where G-d refused Moses' offer to be blotted out from His book, He accepted Jesus' choice to step forward and take the sins of the world on His shoulders.

Moses was not an officiating priest, but his brother, Aaron, was. On earth, Jesus was not an officiating priest either, but He is today in heaven.[146] Therefore, just as Moses was atop Mt. Sinai, pleading for the release from judgement of the Jewish people, Jesus now advocates for the release of sinners from judgement on the basis of His sacrificial death.[147] In the Christian New Testament, it says in the book of Hebrews:

> G-d, after He spoke long ago to the fathers in the prophets in many portions and in many ways, in these last days has spoken to us in *His* Son whom He appointed heir of all things, through whom also He made the world. And He is the radiance of His glory and the exact representation of His nature, and upholds all things by the word of His power. When He had made purification of sins, He sat down at the right hand of the Majesty on High; . . .
>
> For this reason we must pay much closer attention to what we have heard, lest we drift away *from it*. For if the word spoken through angels proved unalterable, and every

---

[145] Heb. 3:1-6.

[146] Acts 1:9-11; Eph. 1:20.

[147] 1 Jn. 2:1-2. Although Jesus is not a descendant of Aaron, He is a High Priest in heaven through the order of Melchizedek. We will cover this subject in Volume 4.

transgression and disobedience received a just recompense, how shall we escape if we neglect so great a salvation?[148]

and,

> . . . He is able to save forever those who draw near to G-d through Him, since He always lives to make intercession for them.
>
> For it was fitting that we should have such a high priest, holy, innocent, undefiled, separated from sinners and exalted above the heavens; who does not need daily, like those high priests, to offer up sacrifices, first for His own sins, and then for the *sins* of the people, because this He did once for all when He offered up Himself.[149]

Jesus was an innocent man. Therefore, He did not need a sacrifice for sins. But rather, through His death, He was able to pay the price of justice for the sins of another. But even beyond that, He was G-d who came down and took the form of a man. As such, He was infinite, and His death could pay the price for the sins of more than just one other person. In fact, He had the capacity to pay the price for the sins of the entire world.[150] Jesus is the G-d-sized solution for the ocean of evil perpetrated by us down through the ages. In Jesus is the answer to the paradox of Exodus 34:7. For, thanks to Jesus' sacrificial death, G-d is able to both serve justice and offer forgiveness at the same time. This is G-d's magnificent

---

[148] Heb. 1:1-3; 2:1-3a.
[149] Heb. 7:25-27.
[150] Heb. 1:1-2:4; 4:14-16; 7:25-28; 10:11-22.

solution to our problem. The author of Hebrews is beseeching us not to be dismissive of it.

One of Jesus' statements that reveals that His heart for sinners was the same as Moses' was mentioned in the previous chapter of this book. Namely, as the Roman soldiers were pounding spikes through his hands and feet, Jesus said: "Father, forgive them; for they do not know what they are doing."[151] Here is another statement showing Jesus' heart for the lost: "Now My soul has become troubled; and what shall I say, 'Father, save Me from this hour'? But for this purpose I came to this hour."[152] Despite the terrible cost, Jesus would not be deterred from paying the price of justice for the guilty. In His words, in His actions, and in His heart, Jesus extended grace and forgiveness to mankind.

*   *   *   *   *

There are also other parallels between Moses and Jesus. One has to do with their births. Both of them were sought by kings to be murdered: Moses by the Egyptian pharaoh, and Jesus by Herod the Great. In Moses' case, his life was not specifically sought, but rather he was to be killed along with all the other Jewish baby boys. Pharaoh had grown fearful of the Jews because of their large numbers; therefore, he issued this order of death.[153] In Jesus' case, King Herod feared Him, for he heard that Jesus was to become the king of the Jews. Thus, he ordered all the Jewish baby boys in and around Bethlehem to be killed in an attempt to get rid of Jesus.[154] Thanks to the swift action of both Moses' and Jesus' parents, as well as the hand of G-d, both survived.

---

[151] Lk. 23:34.
[152] Jn. 12:27.
[153] Ex. 1:15-22.
[154] Lk. 2:1-18.

Moses and Jesus were also alike in that just as Moses spoke to G-d regularly to draw on His help to lead the Jewish people, so too did Jesus. Jesus was known for withdrawing to spend time in prayer with G-d.[155]

Another similarity between Moses and Jesus is that just as the Jews caught a glimpse of G-d when they saw the glory of G-d shining forth on Moses' face, so too did the Jews who came into contact with Jesus behold the glory of G-d. As Jesus walked among us, He revealed G-d to us by His words and deeds.[156] His face displayed the glory of G-d, but not by glowing supernaturally. Rather, the people He encountered witnessed the smile of G-d, a smile born of true love for all people.

* * * * *

Moses is also a type of the Messiah in that Moses was G-d's chosen deliverer of the Jews. He led them from slavery in Egypt to freedom and prosperity in Israel. When Jesus comes back, He will fulfill this role. He will put an end to the wicked Gentile empire that will arise and oppress the rest of the world at the end of time.[157] Then He will gather the Jews from the four corners of the earth and bring them back to their land.[158] Further, He will establish peace across the earth.[159] Psalm 2 puts it this way regarding the destruction of the Gentile enemy forces: "Thou shalt break them with a rod of iron, Thou shalt shatter them like earthenware."[160] This is a quote from G-d to the Messiah. Imagine a strong man smashing clay pots with a rod of iron. The pots do not stand a chance. This is what will

---

[155] Mt. 18:23; Lk. 6:12.

[156] Jn. 1:14.

[157] Ps.2; Dan. 2:44–45; Mt. 24:22.

[158] Isa. 11:11-12; Ezek. 36-37.

[159] Isa. 9:6-7 (5-6); Zech. 9:10.

[160] Ps. 2:9.

happen to the armies of man when they come up against G-d and His Messiah.[161] In Isaiah chapter 9, Isaiah describes the Messiah's visit to earth at the end of time as follows:

> Thou shalt multiply the nation, Thou shalt increase their gladness; they will be glad in Thy presence as with the gladness of harvest, as men rejoice when they divide the spoil. For Thou shalt break the yoke of their burden and the staff on their shoulders, the rod of their oppressor, as at the battle of Midian. For every boot of the booted warrior in the *battle* tumult, and cloak rolled in blood, will be for burning, fuel for the fire. For a child will be born to us, a son will be given to us; and the government will rest on His shoulders; and His name will be called Wonderful Counselor, Mighty G-d, Eternal Father, Prince of Peace. There will be no end to the increase of *His* government or of peace, on the throne of David and over his kingdom, to establish it and to uphold it with justice and righteousness from then on and forevermore. The zeal of the L-rd of hosts will accomplish this.[162]

The Jews have not been aggressors in history. Never once did they seek to conquer so much as an acre beyond the borders G-d prescribed for them. Yet, they have been attacked, conquered, exiled, occupied, and victimized time and again by hostile Gentile regimes over the last four

---

[161] Ps. 2:2.
[162] Isa. 9:3-7 (2-6).

thousand years. They have been beaten with rods wielded by the Egyptians, Midianites, Assyrians, Babylonians, Greeks, Romans, Catholics, Russians, Nazis, Islamic extremists, et al. G-d allowed some of these attacks to succeed as the Jews trampled on His warnings and threw off His protection.[163]

At the end of history, the armies of the entire world will gather in Israel to wreak havoc one more time against the Jewish people. But they will fail as the Messiah will wield a rod of iron and smash this vast assemblage of troops like so many clay pots. Isaiah wrote that the Messiah is G-d, and yet that He would also come down to earth and be born as a man, a Jewish man of the line of David. The Messiah came the first time, two thousand years ago, and He was Jesus. When He returns, He will not come as a man, but rather as Mighty G-d.[164] After executing justice and delivering the Jews, He will bring peace to the earth. Never again will the Jews receive judgement from G-d, and never again will they be attacked and conquered by a hostile foreign power.[165] Hallelujah! In the words of G-d:

> "For a brief moment I forsook you, but with great compassion I will gather you. In an outburst of anger I hid My face from you for a moment; but with everlasting kindness I will have compassion on you," says the L-rd your Redeemer.[166]

---

163 Zech. 7:11-12.
164 Mt. 24:3, 30-31. Rev. 19:11-18.
165 Isa. 12; 51:17-23; 54:7-13; 61:1-3.
166 Isa. 54:7-8.

12

DAVID'S ACT OF UNCONDITIONAL LOVE

Jonathan was David's best friend, and he was a very faithful friend. He stood against his father's sin, and he even graciously accepted the loss of his own opportunity to be the next king. For, his father was King Saul. In 1 Samuel 18 is the story of the genesis of Saul's jealousy of David. Of course, it was never good to be the object of the king's jealousy. Needless to say, Saul's emotions got the better of him, and he called for David to be killed.[167] But Jonathan warned David. Sometime later, in 1 Samuel 20, David and Jonathan discussed a plan to detect if Saul was still intent on taking David's life or whether he had calmed down and changed his mind. Eventually their conversation shifted and they renewed a pact they had made earlier:

---

[167] 1 Sam. 19:1.

> Then Jonathan said to David, "The L-rd, the
> G-d of Israel, be witness! When I have
> sounded out my father about this time
> tomorrow, or the third day, behold, if there is
> good feeling toward David, shall I not then
> send to you and make it known to you? If it
> please my father to do you harm, may the
> L-rd do so to Jonathan and more also, if I do
> not make it known to you and send you away,
> that you may go in safety. And may the L-rd
> be with you as He has been with my father.
> And if I am still alive, will you not show me
> the lovingkindness of the L-rd, that I may not
> die? And you shall not cut off your
> lovingkindness from my house forever, not
> even when the L-rd cuts off every one of the
> enemies of David from the face of the earth."
> So Jonathan made a covenant with the house
> of David, saying, "May the L-rd require it at
> the hands of David's enemies." And Jonathan
> made David vow again because of his love for
> him, because he loved him as he loved his
> own life.[168]

Jonathan vowed not to double-cross David or lead him
into a trap. David vowed not to do harm to Jonathan or his
house once David's day came and G-d installed him as the
king of Israel.

Saul's anger and jealousy still burned against David, and
Jonathan did indeed let David know. Of course, the events
that took place in the years that followed in which David and
his mighty men were on the run from Saul are well known. So

---

[168] 1 Sam. 20:12-17.

too, the event in which Jonathan and Saul died side by side in battle against the Philistines is also well known.[169]

Jonathan was many things, and they were all good. He was loyal, humble, godly, brave, and also prescient, for sure enough, the day came when David was king. In the ancient world, and even in the modern world, when a new king or ruler takes the seat of power, any potential competitor better flee, lest they lose their life. This would include all the remaining family members of the previous king. Hence, Jonathan made David vow to spare him and his house once David became king. Unfortunately, Jonathan was not alive to see that day, but he had one son who was. Herein lies one of the lesser-known events of David's life, the sad story of Mephibosheth.

Mephibosheth was five years old on the day his father, grandfather, and uncles all died. On that day, Mephibosheth's nursemaid grabbed him and fled, fearing for his life. In her rush, there was an accident and Mephibosheth became crippled.[170] It was not good to be disabled in the ancient world as there were no such things as handicap-accessible buildings, transportation, or jobs. But on top of that, Mephibosheth feared for his life. In fact, he wound up moving to Lo-debar, which was a desolate place where one might go to get lost.

At some point later, it occurred to David to inquire as to whether there were any surviving family members of the late King Saul:

> Then David said, "Is there yet anyone left of the house of Saul, that I may show him kindness for Jonathan's sake?" Now there was a servant of the house of Saul whose

---

[169] 1 Sam. 31:1-6.
[170] 2 Sam. 4:4.

name was Ziba, and they called him to David; and the king said to him, "Are you Ziba?" And he said, "*I am* your servant." And the king said, "Is there not yet anyone of the house of Saul to whom I may show the kindness of G-d?" And Ziba said to the king, "There is still a son of Jonathan who is crippled in both feet." So the king said to him, "Where is he?" And Ziba said to the king, "Behold, he is in the house of Machir the son of Ammiel in Lo-debar." Then King David sent and brought him from the house of Machir the son of Ammiel, from Lo-debar. And Mephibosheth, the son of Jonathan the son of Saul, came to David and fell on his face and prostrated himself. And David said, "Mephibosheth." And he said, "Here is your servant!" And David said to him, "Do not fear, for I will surely show kindness to you for the sake of your father Jonathan, and will restore to you all the land of your grandfather Saul; and you shall eat at my table regularly. Again he prostrated himself and said, "What is your servant, that you should regard a dead dog like me?"

Then the king called Saul's servant Ziba, and said to him, "All that belonged to Saul and to all his house I have given to your master's grandson. And you and your sons and your servants shall cultivate the land for him, and you shall bring in *the produce* so that your master's grandson may have food; nevertheless Mephibosheth your master's grandson shall eat at my table regularly."

Now Ziba had fifteen sons and twenty
servants. Then Ziba said to the king,
"According to all that my lord the king
commands his servant so your servant will
do." So Mephibosheth ate at David's table as
one of the king's sons. And Mephibosheth
had a young son whose name was Mica. And
all who lived in the house of Ziba were
servants to Mephibosheth. So Mephibosheth
lived in Jerusalem, for he ate at the king's
table regularly. Now he was lame in both
feet.[171]

What a beautiful story. Right after Ziba identified himself,
David said: "Is there not yet anyone of the house of Saul to
whom I may show the kindness of G-d?"[172] In the Hebrew, the
last phrase, "the kindness of G-d," is actually one word. It is
the word, ḥesed; and it refers to the special love that G-d has
for people. David knew G-d's ḥesed well. There are a number
of passages in which he used this word to write about G-d's
love. For example, in Psalm 103:11-12, David wrote, "For as
high as the heavens are above the earth, so great is His love
for those who fear Him; as far as the east is from the west, so
far has He removed our transgressions from us."[173] In Psalm
51, David wrote about turning to G-d for mercy despite his
great sin with Bathsheba. Verse 1 (3) says, "Have mercy on me,
O G-d, according to Your unfailing love; according to Your
great compassion blot out my transgressions."[174] In these

---

[171] 2 Sam. 9.

[172] 2 Sam. 9:3a.

[173] This is the translation in the NIV Bible: Kenneth L. Barker et
al., eds., *NIV Study Bible* (Grand Rapids: Zondervan, 1985, 1995, 2002)
903.

[174] Ibid., p. 842.

passages, ḥesed is translated as "the kindness of G-d," "love," and "unfailing love." Indeed, G-d's love is greater than ours. It has to do with deep kindness, forgiveness, and compassion. His love is both emotional and active. This word is not just another synonym for the word 'love' as we know it today in our culture. It is a technical term that teaches us about who G-d is and how He relates to us. Surely David used this word intentionally in 2 Samuel 9 where he wanted to extend this kind of love to someone from the house of Saul.[175]

Thus, David's interaction with Mephibosheth is symbolic of G-d's dealings with us. David initiated this encounter with Mephibosheth just as G-d initiates with us. Surely, we do not seek Him out. We are lost, and He comes and reaches out to us. David was the king of Israel, which at the time, was a powerful nation. Mephibosheth was crippled in both feet. He could not even use crutches. Mephibosheth was hiding in fear for his life in Lo-debar. He viewed himself as a "dead dog,"[176] and in a sense, he was right. That was his standing in life. Yet David wanted to be resolved with him as one of the last remaining members of the house of Saul. In our case, the G-d of the Jews is the one true G-d, and we are mere specks riding around on planet Earth. Furthermore, not only are we tiny in stature, but we have each sinned and are morally unfit to come before G-d. Yet, G-d wants to resolve His differences with us and form a relationship with each of us!

But David did not just grant Mephibosheth the legal position of amnesty. He went far beyond that as he restored all of Saul's fortune to him. But that was not even necessary, for David welcomed him to live in Jerusalem and eat at the king's table. Indeed, Mephibosheth was treated the same way

---

[175] Dennis McCallum, Bible teaching, "Mephibosheth (2 Sam. 9)," 9/1/2005, https://teachings.dwellcc.org/teaching/163 (accessed May 5, 2022).

[176] 2 Sam. 9:8.

as David treated his own children.[177] So too, G-d has a plan to atone for our sins and welcome us into His presence as His adoptive children.[178] One additional noteworthy feature is that David was faithful to his covenantal promise to Jonathan despite Saul's multiyear effort to kill him.[179] So too, G-d made covenantal promises to Abraham to bring forth from him a "great nation,"[180] and to bless "all the families of the earth"[181] through him and his descendants. Certainly, G-d will be faithful to His promises despite the Jews' and our rebellions.[182]

This story bears a strong resemblance to many interactions that Jesus had with sinful people He came across in His ministry. Furthermore, the word 'ḥesed' from the Hebrew Bible is virtually identical in meaning to the Greek word 'charis' from the Christian New Testament. Charis is an important word in the Christian New Testament, and it is typically translated as "grace." It is the word from which our English word 'charity' is derived. The reason for that is because G-d's forgiveness is a gift; it is wholly undeserved. In Luke chapter 15 is an example of Jesus exhibiting this gracious love towards sinful people:

> Now all the tax-gatherers and the sinners were coming near Him to listen to Him. And both the Pharisees and the scribes *began* to grumble, saying, "This man receives sinners and eats with them."

---

[177] 2 Sam. 9:11.
[178] Lk. 15:11-32; Rom. 8:15; Eph. 1:5.
[179] 2 Sam. 9:7.
[180] Gen. 12:2.
[181] Gen. 12:3.
[182] Gen. 15:9-17.

And He told this parable, saying, "What man among you, if he has a hundred sheep and has lost one of them, does not leave the ninety-nine in the open pasture, and go after the one which is lost, until he finds it? And when he has found it, he lays it on his shoulders, rejoicing. And when he comes home, he calls together his friends and his neighbors, saying to them, 'Rejoice with me, for I have found my sheep which was lost!' I tell you that in the same way, there will be *more* joy in heaven over one sinner who repents, than over ninety-nine righteous persons who need no repentance.
. . ."

And He said, "A certain man had two sons; and the younger of them said to his father, 'Father, give me the share of the estate that falls to me.' And he divided his wealth between them. And not many days later, the younger son gathered everything together and went on a journey into a distant country, and there he squandered his estate with loose living. Now when he had spent everything, a severe famine occurred in that country, and he began to be in need. And he went and attached himself to one of the citizens of that country, and he sent him into his fields to feed swine. And he was longing to fill his stomach with the pods that the swine were eating, and no one was giving *anything* to him. But when he came to his senses, he said, 'How many of my father's hired men have more than enough bread, but I am dying here with hunger! I will get up and go to my father, and will say to him, "Father, I have sinned against heaven, and in your sight; I am no longer worthy to be called your son; make me as one of your hired men."' And he got up and came to his father. But while he was still a long way off, his father saw him, and felt compassion *for him*, and ran and embraced him, and kissed him. And the son said to him, 'Father, I have sinned against heaven, and in your sight; I am no longer worthy to be called your son; make me as one of your hired men."' But the father said to his slaves, 'Quickly bring out the best robe and put it on him, and put a ring on his hand and sandals on his feet; and bring the fattened calf, kill it, and let us eat and be merry; for this son of mine was dead, and has come to life again; he was lost, and has been found.' And they began to be merry. Now his older son was in the field, and when he came and approached the house, he heard music and dancing. And he summoned one of the servants and *began* inquiring what these things might be. And he said to him, 'Your brother has come, and your father has killed the fattened calf, because he has received him back safe and sound.' But he became angry, and was not willing to go in; and his father came out and *began* entreating him. But he answered and said to his father, 'Look! For so many years I have been serving you, and I have never neglected a command of yours; and yet you have never given me a kid, that I might be merry with my friends;

but when this son of yours came, who has devoured your wealth with harlots, you killed the fattened calf for him.' And he said to him, '*My* child, you have always been with me, and all that is mine is yours. But we had to be merry and rejoice, for this brother of yours was dead and *has begun* to live, and *was* lost and has been found.'"[183]

Here we see Jesus' heart. Tax-gatherers sided with the Romans and betrayed their people for money. Needless to say, they were loathed by the rest of Jewish society. Similarly, the term 'sinners' refers to those who had given themselves over to sin and were condemned by society. For example, prostitutes were considered to be sinners. Nonetheless, Jesus did not treat them judgmentally. Rather, He treated them like human beings. He ate meals with them and showed them acceptance. Jesus' behavior caused the religious leaders in society to grumble. Sometimes I grumble. People around me do not care for it when I act this way. Surely, the tax-gatherers and sinners did not want to go anywhere near the Pharisees and scribes. For, the religious leaders were judgmental. On the other hand, Jesus was full of grace and kindness.

Jesus tried to explain his actions to the Pharisees and scribes in the parables above. In the first parable, Jesus likens a sinful person to a sheep who has lost its way. The shepherd loves the sheep and searches for the lost sheep. Upon finding the sheep, the shepherd gently carries it home and is relieved and joyous. The shepherd does not scold the sheep, but rather is warm and loving towards his sheep. Then the shepherd shares the good news with his friends and celebrates the recovery of his sheep. The idea that this could be G-d's attitude

---

[183] Lk. 15:1-7, 11-32.

towards sinful people was antithetical to the way the religious people thought. Jesus was trying to get them to see that G-d seeks out those who are lost. G-d wants people who have acted shamefully to turn to Him and turn their lives around. When a sinful person turns back in this fashion, this brings G-d great joy, and He welcomes them back and receives them with lovingkindness.

In the next parable, the parable of the Prodigal Son, Jesus goes into greater detail to make sure we understand that G-d loves us and cares for our well-being despite our sin. The sinfulness of the younger son is not downplayed, and it is extraordinary. But the love of the father is greater! This son rudely asked for his inheritance early, and then went out and squandered it as he slept with prostitutes. He did not value being the beloved son of a very good man who treated his workers well. This young fool just wanted to live it up as he responded to the call of sin. But finally, he ran out of money and became poor. Then he saw the error of his ways. So, he went back to his father and apologized to see if he could get a job and provide for himself. Rightfully did the son declare to his father, "I have sinned against heaven and in your sight; I am no longer worthy to be called your son." But the only thing his dad cared about was being reunited with him. Of course, this is true. Parents love their children and will do whatever they can to help them find their way in life. In fact, this foolish young man's dad had been waiting for him to return. Indeed, G-d has his eye on each of us, and He is waiting for us to be ready to hear His call! It is not that our sins do not matter, for they do. But, G-d's love for us is shocking. Jesus came to pay the price of justice in our place. Now, G-d, like this father, is free to pour blessings down upon those who receive His offer of salvation.

The older brother in this parable represents the religious in society. On one level, their moral behavior is laudable, and they cause much less trouble and hurt to others than sinful people do. But the dirty little secret is that their hearts are not pure. They are not gracious like G-d is. They feel little to no joy when a sinful person turns to G-d and is blessed by Him. Their behavior is guided by their desire to reap a reward. They do not behave well simply because they understand that G-d is their loving heavenly father and they want to enjoy a two-way love relationship with Him.

Some of us are overtly sinful, like the prodigal son, and some of us are not. Many of us are trying our best to live good lives. Yet, none of us is perfect.[184] G-d looks down upon us, and He smiles.[185] He just loves us. He sees our moral filth, but He sees the good in us too. He wants to be reconciled with us for our sakes, for G-d is full of grace and compassion. But do we want to be reconciled to Him? Are we willing to turn to Him and receive Jesus' offer of salvation?

---

[184] Isa. 53:6; Rom. 3:23.
[185] Psalm 139.

13

DANIEL'S EMERGENCE FROM THE LIONS' DEN

Daniel was very godly. Even in the face of death, he would not compromise his faith. Daniel had been taken hostage to Babylon as a young man where he was being groomed to become an assistant to King Nebuchadnezzar. However, he refused to eat and drink the rich food and wine from the king's table as it had been dedicated to pagan deities.[186] He requested of the commander of the officials that he and three of his companions be given only vegetables and water. Daniel further proposed a trial period of ten days for them to consume this diet to see if they would lose weight. The commander feared that if they started looking gaunt, the king would be displeased. Then the king would have him killed, as the commander was in charge of all of the youths in the

---

[186] John F. Walvoord, *Daniel the Key to Prophetic Revelation* (Chicago: The Moody Bible Insti-tute, 1971) 37.

program including Daniel and his three friends. After all, King Nebuchadnezzar was an absolute monarch who had no tolerance for anything short of complete obedience. Nonetheless, the commander said 'OK' to Daniel's test. G-d blessed Daniel, and he and his three friends looked healthy despite their meager diet at the end of the ten days. It is notable that when Daniel proposed his test, he did not say that if they started losing weight, then he would eat the king's food. Rather, then Daniel would accept the consequences, but no matter what, he was not going to compromise his faith and eat the unclean food.[187]

Many decades later, Daniel was in a similar situation. But he still was determined to follow G-d no matter what. This story is recorded in Daniel chapter 6. At this point in time, the Babylonian Empire was over and the Persian Empire had begun:

> It seemed good to Darius to appoint 120 satraps over the kingdom, that they should be in charge of the whole kingdom, and over them three commissioners (of whom Daniel was one), that these satraps might be accountable to them, and that the king might not suffer loss. Then this Daniel began distinguishing himself among the commissioners and satraps because he possessed an extraordinary spirit, and the king planned to appoint him over the entire kingdom. Then the commissioners and satraps began trying to find a ground of accusation against Daniel in regard to government affairs; but they could find no

---

[187] Dan. 1:13.

ground of accusation or *evidence* of corruption, inasmuch as he was faithful, and no negligence or corruption was *to be* found in him. Then these men said, 'We shall not find any ground of accusation against this Daniel unless we find it against him with regard to the law of his G-d." Then these commissioners and satraps came by agreement to the king and spoke to him as follows: "King Darius, live forever! All the commissioners of the kingdom, the prefects and the satraps, the high officials and the governors have consulted together that the king should establish a statue and enforce an injunction that anyone who makes a petition to any god or man besides you, O king, for thirty days, shall be cast into the lions' den. Now, O king, establish the injunction and sign the document so that it may not be changed, according to the law of the Medes and Persians, which may not be revoked." Therefore King Darius signed the document, that is, the injunction.

Now when Daniel knew that the document was signed, he entered his house (now in his roof chamber he had windows open toward Jerusalem); and he continued kneeling on his knees three times a day, praying and giving thanks before his G-d, as he had been doing previously.[188]

---

[188] Dan. 6:1-10.

Needless to say, these men spied on Daniel, caught him in the act of praying to G-d, and turned him in to the king.

> Then, as soon as the king heard this statement, he was deeply distressed and set *his* mind on delivering Daniel; and even until sunset he kept exerting himself to rescue him. Then these men came by agreement to the king and said to the king, "Recognize, O king, that it is a law of the Medes and Persians that no injunction or statute which the king establishes may be changed."
>
> Then the king gave orders, and Daniel was brought in and cast into the lions' den. The king spoke and said to Daniel, "Your G-d whom you constantly serve will Himself deliver you." And a stone was brought and laid over the mouth of the den; and the king sealed it with his own signet ring and with the signet rings of his nobles, so that nothing might be changed in regard to Daniel. Then the king went off to his palace and spent the night fasting, and no entertainment was brought before him; and his sleep fled from him.
>
> Then the king arose with the dawn, at the break of day, and went in haste to the lions' den. And when he had come near the den to Daniel, he cried out with a troubled voice. The king spoke and said to Daniel, "Daniel, servant of the living G-d, has your G-d, whom you constantly serve, been able to deliver you from the lions?" Then Daniel spoke to the king, "O king, live forever! My G-d sent His

angel and shut the lions' mouths, and they have not harmed me, inasmuch as I was found innocent before Him; and also toward you, O king, I have committed no crime." Then the king was very pleased and gave orders for Daniel to be taken up out of the den. So Daniel was taken up out of the den, and no injury whatever was found on him, because he had trusted in his G-d. The king then gave orders, and they brought those men who had maliciously accused Daniel, and they cast them, their children, and their wives into the lions' den; and they had not reached the bottom of the den before the lions overpowered them and crushed all their bones.

Then Darius the king wrote to all the peoples, nations, and *men of every* language who were living in all the land: "May your peace abound! I make a decree that in all the dominion of my kingdom men are to fear and tremble before the G-d of Daniel; for He is the living G-d and enduring forever, and His kingdom is one which will not be destroyed, and His dominion *will be* forever. He delivers and rescues and performs signs and wonders in heaven and on earth, who has *also* delivered Daniel from the power of the lions."

So this Daniel enjoyed success in the reign of Darius and in the reign of Cyrus the Persian.[189]

---

[189] Dan. 6:14-28.

Daniel was an exceptional man. He was capable, and he was morally good. Hence, the king was pleased to place him in a very high position of authority. Undoubtedly, the people below Daniel were also pleased, for everyone appreciates a good leader. That is to say, everyone was pleased except the other satraps and commissioners who were jealous of Daniel's success. This is very similar to what Jesus experienced. Huge crowds were following Jesus around listening to Him teach and watching Him heal the lame and the diseased. The Jewish people loved Jesus as they saw in Him the face of G-d, and it was the face of love. The people who did not like Jesus were the religious leaders in Judea who were jealous of his success.[190] No large crowds were following them around, and nor were they receiving an exuberant response. After all, the religious leaders in that day were preaching a message of following the Law meticulously; and they themselves were living very rules-oriented lives. Such a message may appeal to some, but it will never engender a response like the one Jesus was getting. Furthermore, the religious leaders were offended by Jesus because He disagreed with their legalistic approach to the Law. His focus was on approaching G-d in the way that David did, as a person.

In verse 4 (5) of Daniel 6, it says: "Then the commissioners and satraps began trying to find a ground of accusation against Daniel in regard to government affairs; but they could find no ground of accusation or *evidence of corruption*, . . ." So too, the religious leaders in the first century CE sought to have Jesus taken off the stage in the same way. Multiple times they attempted to set Him up to either discredit Him with the Jews or get Him in trouble with the Romans. Here is an example:

---

[190] Mt. 27:18.

Then the Pharisees went and counseled
together how they might trap Him in what He
said. And they sent their disciples to Him,
along with the Herodians, saying, "Teacher,
we know that You are truthful and teach the
way of G-d in truth, and defer to no one; for
You are not partial to any. Tell us therefore,
what do You think? Is it lawful to give a poll-
tax to Caesar, or not?" But Jesus perceived
their malice, and said, "Why are you testing
Me, you hypocrites? Show Me the coin *used*
for the poll-tax." And they brought Him a
denarius. And He said to them, "Whose
likeness and inscription is this?" They said to
Him, "Caesar's." Then He said to them, "Then
render to Caesar the things that are Caesar's;
and to G-d the things that are G-d's." And
hearing *this*, they marveled, and leaving Him,
they went away.[191]

They gave up, for Jesus was too smart to fall for their
traps. Furthermore, He was innocent and righteous. They did
not understand that there would be two comings of the
Messiah. Jesus was not worried about the illicit Roman
occupation at His first coming. He will take care of that when
He returns. He came the first time to make atonement for our
sins and lead us to G-d. Thus, His answer.

The religious leaders could not trap Jesus in this
encounter, but the commissioners and satraps were able to
trick King Darius. They got him to sign an injunction saying
that, for the next thirty days, the people must bow down to
him alone. He was a good king, but he thought too highly of

---

[191] Mt. 22:15-22.

himself and he made a mistake. For, he had no right to sign such a document. Of course, Daniel was not going to bow down to the king, and nor was he going to stop praying to G-d. So Daniel was in trouble, for the way it worked back then was that once a king in the Medo-Persian Empire signed an injunction, it could not be rescinded. Darius did not want to send Daniel to his death, but once the commissioners and satraps caught Daniel praying to G-d, Darius' hands were tied.

So too were Pontius Pilate's hands tied in such a way that he could not set Jesus free. Unlike King Darius, Pilate had no regard for the G-d of the Jews. Pilate was the Roman procurator or governor of the province of Judea. He was guilty of bringing effigies of Caesar into Jerusalem, which was forbidden under Jewish law. The Jews took a righteous stand and he removed them.[192] Later he laid an ambush against a crowd of Jews who were protesting his commandeering of Temple funds to build an aqueduct. In that event, his soldiers killed "a great number" of Jews.[193] It was around this time that Jesus was brought before him, and although it is clear that he did not want to execute Jesus,[194] his hands were tied in that he was fearful of "imperial displeasure if Tiberius heard of further unrest in Judaea."[195] For, it was the job of the Roman governors to maintain a state of stability and peace throughout all the outlying provinces. Needless to say, it would be very imprudent for a governor to test the Emperor's patience. Thus, Pilate did not want to have a conflict with the Jews over Jesus, whom they were seeking to have crucified.[196]

---

[192] Josephus, *Antiquities* 18.3.1 (55).

[193] Josephus, *Antiquities* 18.3.2 (60-62).

[194] Mt. 27:19; Jn. 19:12.

[195] J. D. Douglas et al., eds., *New Bible Dictionary*, Second Edition, (Wheaton, Il.: Tyndale House Publishers, Inc., 1982, 1984) 940.

[196] Mt. 27:22-24.

Jesus was not just another criminal. Indeed, Jesus was no ordinary man, and Pilate sensed that. Pilate wanted no part in Jesus' death, and he tried multiple times to set Jesus free. But it was not to be. Finally, Pilate gave up; and he made a gesture that would echo down through the ages: ". . . he took water and washed his hands in front of the multitude, saying, 'I am innocent of this Man's blood; see to *that* yourselves.'"[197] Of course, that was not good enough. Neither was what Darius did good enough. They both needed to step up and take whatever consequences may have come their way for doing what is right before G-d. Daniel took such a stand twice in His life. Indeed, at some point, we each must decide whether being faithful to G-d or maintaining our position in society is more important.

Not only did Daniel step up in dramatic moments and take a stand for G-d, but he was also faithful to G-d when no one was looking. He prayed in private every day. One way that Daniel is a type of Jesus is that he was an especially righteous human being. We all sin, even the greatest among us, and Daniel confessed that he was a sinner too.[198] Yet, you could say that, relative to other people, Daniel was free from sin. For, his life was more defined by his faithfulness than by his sins.

One of the ways we know the Bible is true is that, as opposed to other religious scriptures, it tells stories of real people. Certainly, in some of the narratives, G-d intervenes and people experience miracles. But they are real people. So even the greatest and most godly among us, such as King David, have their shameful episodes of sin included in the Bible. But evidently, Daniel's sins were not of this caliber as they are not recorded in the Hebrew Bible. Hence, in his high

---

[197] Mt. 27:24.
[198] Dan. 9:20.

moral character, Daniel is a type of Jesus. For, Jesus was righteous. Of course, righteousness goes beyond the absence of sin, and it entails performing acts of service and speaking words of kindness. Surely, both Daniel and Jesus had wonderful character and were beloved by the people around them. In Jesus' case, no typical human sins or crimes were ascribed to Him by His enemies. The accusation that Jesus' enemies made was that He claimed to be the Messiah:

> Now the chief priests and the whole Council kept trying to obtain false testimony against Jesus, in order that they might put Him to death; and they did not find *any*, even though many false witnesses came forward. But later on two came forward, and said, "This man stated, 'I am able to destroy the temple of G-d and to rebuild it in three days.'" And the high priest stood up and said to Him, "Do You make no answer? What is it that these men are testifying against You?" But Jesus kept silent. And the high priest said to Him, "I adjure You by the living G-d, that You tell us whether You are the Christ, the Son of G-d." Jesus said to him, "You have said it *yourself*; nevertheless I tell you, hereafter you shall see the Son of Man sitting at the right hand of Power, and coming on the clouds of heaven." Then the high priest tore his robes, saying, "He has blasphemed! What further need do we have of witnesses? Behold, you have now heard the blasphemy; what do you think?"

They answered and said, "He is deserving of death!"[199]

Jesus chose not to respond to the two men who misapplied His statement. He did, however, respond to the high priest's question as to whether He was the Messiah or not. He answered by claiming to be the striking figure predicted in Daniel 7:13-14 who will come into G-d's presence and be given glory and rulership of mankind at the end of history. His enemies loathed Him for this answer. They could not accept that Jesus was who He claimed to be. Therefore, the high priest (Caiaphas), the scribes, the elders, the chief priests, and the Sanhedrin proceeded forward and took Jesus to Pilate to be executed.[200]

When it was time for Daniel to serve his sentence, he was put into a lions' den and the opening was covered over with a great stone or boulder. Further, a seal was affixed and imprinted with the king's signet ring and the signet rings of the nobles lest anyone attempt to set Daniel free.

So too with Jesus, once He was crucified, He was laid in a tomb that was a cave hewn out of rock for a rich man named Joseph. Then a large stone was rolled in front of the tomb.[201] The next day, the Jewish religious leaders met with Pilate and urged him to guard the tomb, lest Jesus' disciples take His body and make any outrageous claims as to His resurrection. For, Jesus had predicted that He would rise from the dead after three days similar to the way that Jonah came forth from

---

[199] Mt. 26:59-66.
[200] Mt. 26:57-59.
[201] Mt. 27:57-60.

the belly of a whale after three days.[202] So Pilate installed a guard detail and placed a seal on the stone.[203]

Of course, the main way that Daniel is a type of Jesus is that G-d supernaturally intervened and brought Him out of the lions' den alive. No man stepped up and did the right thing by intervening on Daniel's behalf to save his life, but G-d did. G-d supernaturally closed the lions' mouths, and they left Daniel unharmed. It was an outright miracle. So too with Jesus, G-d intervened, and Jesus was raised from the dead and came out of the tomb alive. G-d brought Jesus back to life after He had been crucified, had a spear thrust into His side to verify that He was dead, and was laid to rest in a tomb for three days. Following this miracle, Jesus would go on to walk amongst us for a period of forty days;[204] and then He ascended into heaven.[205]

In Daniel's case, King Darius could not sleep all night, and he went to check on Daniel early the next day. To his surprise, Daniel was alive. Similarly, in Jesus' case, people who loved Him came to the tomb to see what was going on. Mary Magdalene was one of them. She came early in the morning a few days later. She found that the stone had been moved away from the entrance of the tomb, and she left and went to get Jesus' disciples Peter and John. The three of them came to the tomb and it was empty. However, she had an encounter with Jesus outside the tomb. At first, she thought Jesus was the gardener. Then,

> Jesus said to her, "Mary!" She turned and said to Him in Hebrew "Rabboni!" (which

---

[202] Mt. 12:38-41.
[203] Mt. 27:62-66.
[204] Acts 1:3.
[205] Acts 1:9-11.

means, Teacher). Jesus said to her, "Stop clinging to Me, for I have not yet ascended to the Father; but go to My brethren, and say to them, 'I ascend to My Father and your Father, and My G-d and your G-d.'" Mary Magdalene came, announcing to the disciples, "I have seen the L-rd," and *that* He had said these things to her.

When therefore it was evening, on that day, the first *day* of the week, and when the doors were shut where the disciples were, for fear of the Jews, Jesus came and stood in their midst, and said to them, "Peace be with you." And when He had said this, He showed them both His hands and His side. The disciples therefore rejoiced when they saw the L-rd.[206]

Following Daniel's release from the lions' den, justice was swift and harsh for the criminals who set him up. It was tragic. Even their wives and children paid the ultimate price along with them because of their attempt to advance themselves by getting rid of Daniel. There is a parallel in Jesus' day, but it is somewhat different. Justice was not swift. It took nearly forty years before it was carried out. In the interim, every Jew was invited to turn to Jesus for the forgiveness of their sins including their participation in His death, and many did.[207] Indeed, Christianity is a branch of Judaism that was begun by Jewish people. Of course, most of the Jews spurned Jesus' offer. Tragically, justice for Jesus' wrongful execution came upon the Jews in 70 CE. The suffering was great during the

---

[206] Jn. 20:16-20.
[207] Acts 2:22-41.

siege and eventual bloodbath that took place once the Roman soldiers breached the wall and rushed into Jerusalem. Of course, the long-term suffering of the Jews in the Diaspora has been incalculable as well. Jesus predicted the fall of Jerusalem and the suffering of the Jews, and His heart broke for them.[208]

The final parallel between Daniel's story of deliverance and Jesus' resurrection is that in both events there was a message about G-d that needed to be told to everyone in the world. The G-d of the Jews is the one true G-d, and He is a G-d who delivers. In Daniel's case, G-d delivered him from a den full of lions. In Jesus' case, G-d delivered Him from the grave. In Daniel chapter 6, it says that Darius sent word to "all the peoples, nations, and *men of every* language" about Daniel's G-d who delivered him. So too, Jesus commissioned His followers to take the message of His sacrificial death and resurrection to all the peoples throughout the earth.[209]

* * * * *

Ironically, Daniel chapter 6 is frequently misunderstood. It is often relegated to presentation as a children's story with pictures of cute, gentle lions smiling at Daniel. Upon first reading this story, it may appear incongruous or out of place with the rest of this book, which consists of magnificent prophecy. However, if you think about it, it only makes sense that G-d would foreshadow something as significant as the resurrection of Jesus. In that light, chapter 6 does fit in with the rest of the book, which predicts the important events of history from that time forward.

Indeed, Jesus' resurrection has great meaning because He claimed to be G-d. If Jesus simply perished and underwent

---

[208] Lk. 19:41-44.
[209] Mt. 28:18-20.

burial like everyone else, then His claim to be G-d would not carry much weight. That is why it was foreshadowed by Daniel as well as by Jonah when he was confined in the belly of a whale for three days.[210] When Jesus emerged alive from the tomb, it was undeniable proof to all who saw Him that He really was who He claimed to be. But even for those of us who did not get to see Him in His resurrected state, the resurrection is still proof. After all, His tomb was protected by a guard detail of Rome, and yet, Jesus' body was gone. Furthermore, Jesus' body was never found by anyone despite the fact that His enemies desperately wanted to put an end to all of the fuss over Him. In addition, decades later, all of His disciples, except John, went to their deaths rather than recant that He rose from the dead. In John's case, he was imprisoned but not executed. Jesus' disciples claimed to personally see Him alive after He was killed. If they were lying, why would they all go their deaths rather than recant? No one does that. There is no good alternative explanation for what happened to Jesus' body other than that He resurrected.

In summary, the circumstances leading up to the events of Daniel chapter 6 parallel the circumstances leading up to Jesus' crucifixion. Daniel was a good, moral man, and Jesus was righteous. They were both brave, and neither of them would compromise their faith, even if it meant that they would die. They both had a group of detractors who felt threatened by their popularity and who schemed to have them killed. Their enemies schemed well, and both King Darius and Pontius Pilate had their hands tied and could not undo their sentences of death. Daniel was cast into a lions' den, and Jesus' body was placed in a cave. In both cases, great stones were rolled in front of the openings and official governmental seals were affixed to prevent anyone from interfering with the

---

[210] Jon. 1:17-2:10 (2:1-11); Mt. 16:1-4.

official decrees. People who loved them showed up later to see what was happening. G-d acted on their behalves, and both men emerged alive. In Daniel's case, G-d prevented the lions from harming him. In Jesus' case, He resurrected. Once you see the way all of the details line up between these two events, you cannot unsee it. Surely, Daniel is a type of Jesus. Just as Isaac's near sacrificial death foreshadowed Jesus' crucifixion, so too did Daniel's miraculous emergence from the lions' den foreshadow Jesus' resurrection. G-d had these two events recorded multiple centuries before Jesus came along so that when He was crucified, we could see that it was always G-d's plan for the Messiah to come a first time to die as a sacrifice.

14

CYRUS THE DELIVERER

In America, we honor George Washington and Abraham Lincoln as perhaps our two greatest presidents. The first was a great general who won our freedom on the battlefield. Following the war, he established the precedent for the way future presidents were to exercise their power. Namely, presidents were to conduct themselves as elected officials as opposed to unaccountable monarchs.

Abraham Lincoln also had excellent moral character. He believed in human equality, and he freed the slaves. He had a backbone of steel, and he would not fold to criticism or the massive costs of an all-out civil war.

In the ancient world, Cyrus the Great of Persia accomplished similar feats to those of both George Washington and Abraham Lincoln. He was the general who overtook Media to become the dominant power of a two-nation confederacy. He then conquered the Babylonian Empire as well as other lands. In fact, Cyrus established Persia as the largest empire the world had ever known up to that time.

Nonetheless, despite his great power and all of his victories, Cyrus did not rule as an oppressive dictator. Indeed, he was a humanitarian. He believed in freedom of religion, and he ended slavery within the empire. Upon taking the city of Babylon and deposing Belshazzar, the Babylonian king, he issued the Edict of Cyrus, ensuring the rights of the residents of Babylonia as well as all the peoples under his authority. This edict was inscribed on a clay cylinder. A copy of this cylinder was presented to the United Nations by the government of Iran in 1971. It was warmly received by Secretary-General U Thant, who stated:

> ". . . Cyrus displayed the wisdom of respecting the civilizations and peoples whom he "unified" under his sway. He conquered discreetly, sparing capitals, leaders, and officials. His clemency in victory and his understanding of the wishes of the people under his rule were unprecedented in the annals of the ancient Near East.
>
> As can be deduced from the formal text inscribed on this clay cylinder, Cyrus presented himself to the Babylonians as a liberator. He assumed their throne peacefully, restored their temples and freed their subject populations, thus engendering goodwill and justice all around."[211]

---

[211] UN, (14 October 1971), "Statement by Secretary-General, U Thant, at Presentation of Gift from Iran to United Nations, 14 October," [Press Release SG/SM/1553 and HQ/263], https://r.search.yahoo.com/_ylt=AwrJ6y1NCG1ib7IAJipXNyoA;_ylu=

Not long after taking Babylon, Cyrus granted the Jews who were living in exile in Babylonia the right to return to their homeland. The Jews were in exile because they had been rebelling against G-d for centuries. They failed to listen to His prophets, they bowed to the pagan deities of their neighbors, and they cast aside His commandments.[212] G-d had prophesied through Jeremiah that the Jews would be judged for their rebellion against Him. The instrument of that judgement was Nebuchadnezzar, the king of the Babylonians, who would utterly destroy the southern kingdom of Judah and send the survivors into exile. However, Jeremiah also prophesied that their exile would be temporary and last seventy years.[213] Thus, in a specific decree pertaining to the Jews, Cyrus proclaimed: "The L-rd, the G-d of heaven, has given me all the kingdoms of the earth, and He has appointed me to build Him a house in Jerusalem, which is in Judah. Whoever there is among you of all His people, may the L-rd his G-d be with him, and let him go up!"[214] Hence, Cyrus not only decreed the release of the Jews to return to Judah, but he also called for the Temple to be rebuilt. In addition, he provided funding.

In Daniel chapter 5 is the story of King Belshazzar, the Babylonian co-emperor, who resided in the capital at the time

---

Y29sbwNiZjEEcG9zAzMEdnRpZA-
MEc2VjA3Ny/RV=2/RE=1651341517/RO=10/RU=https%3a%2f%2fsearc
h.archives.un.org%2fuploads%2fr%2funited-nations-ar-
chives%2f6%2f0%2fe%2f60e01378f4efade1353c642dc378bc5544138ce0ce
2f3f4cab3a7ad37905a49a%2fS-0882-0002-02-
00001.pdf/RK=2/RS=FlP67mBNobMONgF1bzzJJI48iJQ-,   (accessed
April 30, 2022).

[212] Jer. 25:1-11; Dan. 9:5-11.
[213] Jer. 25:11-12; Dan. 9:15-19.
[214] 2 Chron. 36:23.

of the fall of Babylon. In Belshazzar, we see similar traits to other kings: cowardliness, arrogance, and ungodliness. As the Babylonian Empire was facing the threat posed by the Persian army amassing outside the city walls, Belshazzar decided to throw a party. He recalled that when the Babylonian army ransacked Jerusalem seventy years earlier, they had removed all the gold and silver vessels from the Temple. He thought it would be a good idea for a servant to bring in some of these gold and silver vessels so that they could drink wine from them and toast their pagan gods.

G-d was not pleased. Suddenly, a hand appeared. It was coming out of the wall, and it started writing on the plaster! It wrote the following inscription: MENĒ, MENĒ, TEKĒL, UPHARSIN.[215] This passage is where we get our modern expression, 'the handwriting is on the wall'. The account of this event in Daniel chapter 5 is not mythical, and nor is it metaphorical. But rather, it is the historical record of a miracle.

None of the king's wise men, including astrologers, diviners, and others, were able to read the words or figure out what they meant. The king was quite upset, and the news of the event reached the queen mother's ears. She entered the scene of the failed party and told her son that there used to be a Jew who was full of the wisdom of "the gods."[216] His name was Daniel and he counseled the earlier king, Nebuchadnezzar. Daniel was summoned posthaste. Sure enough, he could read the inscription, and he understood the meaning. The words were "numbered" (twice), "weighed," and "divided."[217] Daniel explained that the inscription meant that: 1. G-d had numbered the days of Belshazzar's kingdom

---

[215] Dan. 5:25.
[216] Dan. 5:11.
[217] Dan. 5:26-28.

and it was about to come to an end; 2. Belshazzar had been weighed on the scales and found wanting; and 3. His kingdom would be divided and given to the Medes and Persians. Daniel also explained that the root cause of this devastating judgment was Belshazzar's failure to honor G-d and his lack of appreciation that it was G-d who gave him his life and his position of power. Belshazzar remembered the treasures of the Temple of G-d, but he forgot G-d. Furthermore, there is no doubt that he treated people the way the arrogant do when they are in a position of absolute power, and G-d had enough.[218]

The city of Babylon was very well fortified, and it was thought to be impregnable. The city wall was massive. It was so wide that chariots could pass one another as they were driven across the top of it. However, there were openings at the base of the wall through which the Euphrates River entered the city. Cleverly, the Persians diverted the river through a canal into a low area. As the water level receded, they waded into the river and through the openings, thereby gaining access to the city. Then they took the city by surprise, and Belshazzar was slain shortly thereafter.

G-d gave the prophet Isaiah a prophecy about Cyrus between 150 to 200 years before Cyrus set foot in the city of Babylon. The prophecy states:

> " . . . *It is I* who says of Jerusalem, 'She shall
> be inhabited!' and of the cites of Judah, 'They
> shall be built.' And I will raise up her ruins
> again. *It is I* who says to the depth of the sea,

---

[218] It should be noted that the events of this chapter, chapter 14, take place before the events of the last chapter. In other words, Daniel was in exile in Babylon on the night it fell to the Medes and Persians. Then, sometime later, Daniel rose to a high position in the Medo-Persian Empire, which led to the events in the last chapter.

'Be dried up!' and I will make rivers dry. *It is I* who says of Cyrus, '*He is* My shepherd! and he will perform all My desire.' And he declares of Jerusalem, 'She will be built,' and of the temple, 'Your foundation will be laid.'"

Thus says the L-rd to Cyrus His anointed, whom I have taken by the right hand, to subdue nations before him, and to loose the loins of kings; to open doors before him so that gates will not be shut: "I will go before you and make the rough places smooth; I will shatter the doors of bronze, and cut through their iron bars. And I will give you the treasures of the darkness, and hidden wealth of secret places, in order that you may know that it is I, the L-rd, the G-d of Israel, who calls you by your name. For the sake of Jacob My servant, and Israel My chosen *one*, I have also called you by your name; I have given you a title of honor though you have not known Me. I am the L-rd, and there is no other; besides Me there is no G-d. I will gird you, though you have not known Me; that men may know from the rising to the setting of the sun that there is no one besides Me. I am the L-rd, and there is no other, . . ."[219]

Notice that a couple hundred years before he showed up, G-d called out the Jews' deliverer by name. G-d can do that as He stands outside of time. How does that work? We do not know. We just know that this is one piece of evidence that G-d is real and He is the G-d of the Jews.

---

[219] Isa. 44:26b–45:6.

Indeed, just as G-d foretold, these events took place. We know this because the Greek historian, Herodotus, recorded this event. Thus, we know that the gates in the outer wall as well as the gates inside the city leading up from the river were made out of bronze, and that they proved to be no major obstacle for the Persians.[220] Due to their overconfidence, the Babylonians failed to lock or guard the gates inside the city. Thus, the Persians walked right through them and entered the city without a fight.[221] The formidable city defenses, which were years in the making, were overcome in the blink of an eye due to bad leadership and arrogance.

Cyrus was not like Belshazzar. Josephus tells us that Cyrus was shown the prophecy about him in the book of Isaiah.[222] In this prophecy, G-d foretold that Cyrus would be a shepherd to the Jews and guide them back from exile to rebuild Jerusalem and the Temple. Sure enough, Cyrus obeyed G-d. He also acknowledged that the G-d of the Jews is the G-d of heaven, and that it was He who gave him the kingdoms of the earth to rule.[223] In addition, Cyrus returned all of the gold and silver treasures that were stolen from the Temple.[224] No, Cyrus was not at all like Belshazzar. He was humble, he did what G-d called him to do, and he ruled his subjects with benevolence.

Accordingly, G-d generously blessed and honored Cyrus. G-d's honor extended even beyond Cyrus' position as world emperor, for Cyrus was the king who initiated the rebuilding

---

[220] Herodotus, *The Histories*, Book 1, Chapter 179, Section 3 and Book 1, Chapter 180, Section 4, A.D. Godley, ed., n.d., https://www.perseus.tufts.edu/hopper/text?doc=Perseus:text:1999.01.0126, (accessed April 29, 2022).

[221] Herodotus Book 1, Chapter 191, Sections 5 and 6.

[222] Josephus, *Antiquities of the Jews* 11.1.1 (3) - 11.1.2 (7).

[223] 2 Chron. 36:23.

[224] Ezra 1:7; 6:3-5.

of the Temple. This is a rare honor. Not even David was permitted this privilege; only Solomon was honored in this way.

*   *   *   *   *

Now let's examine how Cyrus can be considered a type of Jesus. One parallel has to do with their birth stories. In fact, there are interesting similarities between Cyrus, Jesus, and Moses regarding the circumstances surrounding their births. All three were sought by kings to be murdered: Moses, by a pharaoh; Jesus, by Herod the Great; and Cyrus, by Astyages. Astyages was his maternal grandfather as well as the king of the Medes. According to Herodotus, Astyages had a couple dreams that were similar to one another and that disturbed him. The interpretation he was given stated that a child would be born to his daughter and that child would one day take away his kingdom. Of course, he did what kings do. He called on a man named Harpagus to murder the baby at birth. But his order was not carried out. Instead, Harpagus gave Cyrus to a shepherd and received back the shepherd's stillborn son. The shepherd and his wife raised Cyrus. Unfortunately, when Cyrus was ten, the ruse was discovered. However, the king had a change of heart, and he allowed Cyrus to live. Needless to say, that decision wound up costing him his kingdom many years later.

Another similarity between Cyrus and Jesus is that they were both shepherds of the Jewish people. G-d called Cyrus His shepherd in Isaiah; and indeed, he did shepherd the Jews back to the land of Israel. Jesus claimed to be G-d's shepherd not only for the Jews, but also for the Gentiles.[225] His shepherding two thousand years ago consisted of leading people to turn to G-d for forgiveness and become adopted

---

[225] Jn. 10:16.

children of G-d. Jesus was like Cyrus in that He believed in freedom of religion. He did not practice compulsion in regard to His message that the pathway to G-d is through the forgiveness of your sins.[226] He wanted people to hear His message and make a freewill choice to receive Him or not.

Of course, some of the Jews followed Jesus, but most of them rejected Him. Those who followed Him started the Christian movement.[227] Those who rejected Jesus would go on to experience calamity, as a few decades later the Romans would launch an all-out assault on Israel. In 70 CE, Jerusalem would fall following an awful, protracted siege, and the surviving Jews would be sent into exile to live as slaves. Subsequently, the Jews found themselves living as unwelcome guests spread across Europe, Asia, and the Middle East for the next two thousand years. During these years, Jesus has been using Christians to take His offer of salvation to the Gentiles living across the earth. Nonetheless, it was never Jesus' desire for this judgement to befall the Jews.[228] But He knew that the nation as a whole was going to reject Him. Thus, He stated that He will one day return, at which time the Jews will receive Him as their Messiah.[229]

Indeed, it is primarily the second coming of Jesus that Cyrus' life typifies. Cyrus was a military and political deliverer. He conquered the Babylonian Empire and set the Jews free to return to Israel and rebuild the Temple. At Jesus' second coming, He will subdue nations, gather the Jews from the four corners of the earth, and return them to their land.[230] It will be a new age that will start with Jesus shattering the militaries of the world and putting down the rebellion of mankind once

---

[226] Mk. 6:11; Rev. 3:20.

[227] Mt. 28:16-20.

[228] Mt. 23:37-39.

[229] Zech. 12:10; Mt. 24:3 ff.; Lk. 21:25-28; Rev. 1:7.

[230] Isa. 11:11-12; 49:5-13; Ezek. 36-37.

and for all.[231] There will be a glorious Temple,[232] and Jesus will rule as per the model established by Cyrus. Just as Cyrus ruled with uncharacteristic regard for human rights, so too will Jesus rule the world with benevolence and justice.[233]

Another similarity between Cyrus and Jesus is that Jesus, too, will set the world free from a wicked pagan regime. Belshazzar was a godless, sinful man. He and the Babylonians ruled with an iron fist. Cyrus put Belshazzar and his regime down and introduced freedom to both Jews and Gentiles alike. So too, in the end days, it will be a time of great moral and spiritual darkness as the world will be ruled by an exceedingly wicked man, the Antichrist. Of course, he will not be the only conduit of evil as wickedness will permeate all the nations on earth at that time. It will also be a time of war. In fact, the death and destruction that will take place will be greater than at any other time in history. Per Daniel, the epicenter of the conflict will be in Israel as that is where the Antichrist will be when the armies of the world converge on him.[234] Presumably, a nuclear war will be underway. In fact, Jesus prophesied that His return will come at a point in the fighting in which all life on the planet would have been destroyed had He not come back.[235] But He will come back, and He will put a stop to the Antichrist and the other depraved world leaders and their armies. For, they will all rebel against G-d and oppose His people.[236]

The arrogant rulers at the end of time will make the same mistakes that Belshazzar made. They will have no regard for G-d, and they will act immorally. Indeed, they will lead the

---

[231] Ps. 2; Dan. 2:44-45; Zech. 14:1-8; Mt. 24:22; Rev. 19:11-16.

[232] Ezek. 40-43.

[233] Isa. 9:7 (6); 11:3-5; 42:3-4; Zech. 14:9-11.

[234] Dan. 11:44-45.

[235] Mt. 24:22.

[236] Ps. 2; Ezek. 39:3-6; Zech. 14:1-15; Rev. 19:11-21.

people of the world away from G-d through coercion. Prior to the final day of history, they will kill a multitude to attain power. Then Jesus will return and destroy their kingdoms. In the book of Revelation, it describes the lead-up to the final moment of history as follows:

> And I saw heaven opened; and behold, a white horse, and He who sat upon it *is* called Faithful and True; and in righteousness He judges and wages war. And His eyes *are* a flame of fire, and upon His head *are* many diadems; and He has a name written *upon Him* which no one knows except Himself. And *He is* clothed with a robe dipped in blood; and His name is called the Word of G-d. And the armies which are in heaven, clothed in fine linen, white and clean, were following Him on white horses. And from His mouth comes a sharp sword, so that with it He may smite the nations; and He will rule them with a rod of iron; and He treads the wine press of the fierce wrath of G-d, the Almighty. And on His robe and on His thigh He has a name written, "KING OF KINGS, AND L-RD OF L-RDS."[237]

Jesus' disciple John wrote The Revelation as well as The Gospel According to John. In both writings he calls Jesus the Word of G-d.[238] The book of Revelation is a recording of the vision John received of the end of history. John employs heavy symbolism in this book. Thus, Jesus may not actually ride a

---

[237] Rev. 19:11-16.
[238] Jn. 1:1-5.

horse through the air, though, the sky will darken and there will be a "sign" of Jesus for all to see in the sky.[239] The blood on Jesus' robe is a reference to His first coming, in which He bled considerably as a sacrifice for our sins. This time He will come to administer justice and put an end to the state of unfettered evil that humanity will achieve. Judgement of the Gentile kings and their armies will be swift. All of the men perpetrating this unjust war will come to Israel to inflict mass death upon the Jews.[240] But their plan will fail, and the only mass death that will take place will be their own. When Cyrus came to the city of Babylon, the Babylonians relied on their great city wall for protection. But alas, their confidence in the wall was unfounded. So too, the modern weaponry of man, including even nuclear missiles, will be powerless against the "arm of the L-rd."[241] The number of corpses will be massive, and G-d will employ nature to cleanse the land of their flesh.[242]

* * * * *

In Isaiah 45:1, Cyrus is called G-d's "anointed." This is significant. The word for anointed is the Hebrew word 'māshîaḥ', or in other words, 'messiah'. To be anointed means to have oil ceremonially poured on your head signifying that you have become set apart to play a special role for G-d. The word can either be an adjective, or a noun, as is the case in Isaiah 45:1. The word is most frequently used as a title for both King Saul and King David. In a few places it is used prophetically for the Messiah who will one day come to set the world right. In total, the word is used 39 times in the Hebrew

---

[239] Mt. 24:29-30.
[240] Zech. 12:2-3.
[241] Isa. 53:1.
[242] Rev. 19:17-21.

Bible. It is never used for a Gentile, except in this single reference to Cyrus in the book of Isaiah.

Isaiah chapters 40 through 57 comprise a very important part of the Hebrew Bible. This section of scripture is a conglomeration of intertwining prophecies. The main themes are 1. the fact that the G-d of the Jews is the only G-d, and that all others are fictitious; 2. G-d's desire for people to know who He is, and His revelation of His identity through prophecy and His interventions in history on behalf of the Jews; 3. G-d's enabling of Cyrus to put an end to the wicked Babylonian Empire and set His people free; 4. the failure of the Jewish people to collectively be G-d's servant and represent Him to the world; and 5. the success of an unnamed individual servant of G-d to obey G-d, suffer and die, and thereby provide atonement for sin. This section of the Hebrew Bible can be divided into two subsections: chapters 40-48 and 49-57. Cyrus is the central figure of the first subsection. The suffering servant of G-d who is rejected by the Jewish people is the central figure in the second subsection.[243] To feature Cyrus so prominently in the first subsection is significant. It speaks to how humble and open to G-d Cyrus was. In addition, his shepherding of the Jews back to their land gives an indication of what the Messiah will do at the end of human history.

To some Jews, perhaps more so in the ancient world than today, to suggest that a Gentile could be a messiah, chosen by G-d to shepherd the Jewish people back to Jerusalem, would be offensive. But so it is. Perhaps G-d wants the Jews to understand that their honored position before Him is not due to their worthiness, but rather, it is due to His grace. Indeed, in the book of Isaiah, Isaiah goes out of his way to paint a picture of the sinfulness of the Jewish people. Thus, this time G-d did not select a deliverer from within, like Moses, but

---

[243] Isa. 49:7; 53:3.

rather He used a Gentile king to rescue them. So too, at the end of history, it will be Jesus, whom the Jews rejected, who will come back to save them one final time.

That will be quite a day. Isaiah predicted that G-d will anoint Jesus on that day to "comfort all who mourn, to grant those who mourn *in* Zion, giving them a garland instead of ashes, the oil of gladness instead of mourning, the mantle of praise instead of a spirit of fainting."[244] It will be a day to decompress. Two thousand years of extreme hatred and violence against the Jews will be over in an instant. Isaiah also wrote:

> "For a brief moment I forsook you, but with great compassion I will gather you. In an outburst of anger I hid my face from you for a moment; but with everlasting lovingkindness I will have compassion on you," says the L-rd your redeemer.
>
> "For this is like the days of Noah to Me; when I swore that the waters of Noah should not flood the earth again, so I have sworn that I will not be angry with you, nor will I rebuke you. For the mountains may be removed and the hills may shake, but My lovingkindness will not be removed from you, and My covenant of peace will not be shaken," says the L-rd who has compassion on you.[245]

G-d is using emphatic language in these verses. This will happen. G-d will keep all of His promises to the Jews, and one

---

[244] Isa. 61:2b-3a.
[245] Isa. 54:7-10.

day, all the pain and suffering will be completely over.
Hallelujah!

15

BREADCRUMBS

In the classic German fairytale, Hansel left a trail of breadcrumbs when he and his sister went deep into the woods, so they could find their way out. However, birds ate the breadcrumbs and they became lost. Nevertheless, the idea of leaving markers in the woods so that you can find your trail is a good one. The markers just need to be enduring, and they need to stand out enough to be findable.

Could it be that G-d placed a trail of breadcrumbs in the Hebrew Bible so that we could find the Messiah and understand G-d's plan for us? Of course, the G-d of heaven and earth would know just the right markers to leave so that those who are seekers could find His path for us.

There are similarities between things that happened in the lives of Isaac, Joseph, Moses, David, Daniel, and Cyrus and things that happened in Jesus' life. There are also similarities between their characters and Jesus' character. These similar occurrences and character traits are not ordinary things, but rather, they stand out. The similarities are also meaningful as opposed to trivial. Therefore, they appear to have been inserted in the Bible on purpose to catch our attention and confirm that Jesus is the Messiah.

Now let's compare each of these men's lives to Jesus' life and see how strong this apologia is for identifying Jesus as the Messiah. Are the parallels between these men's lives and Jesus' life just interesting coincidences, or are they more than that?

The Sacrifice of Isaac: We did not cover the story of Abraham and Isaac in this unit because we already covered it in the last unit. But certainly, Abraham's near sacrifice of Isaac presaged Jesus' crucifixion in a number of ways.

In Genesis chapter 22 is the story of the sacrifice of Isaac. Some of the details of this event include: Isaac riding on a donkey part of the way to Mt. Moriah; Isaac carrying a bundle of wood the last length of the journey to the site of the sacrifice; and Isaac being bound and placed on the wood to undergo a sacrificial death at the hands of his father.

This series of details is quite similar to the sequence of events of Jesus' crucifixion: Jesus rode a donkey to the gates of Jerusalem; Jesus carried the wooden cross part of the way to the site of His crucifixion, which was at the same location as the near sacrifice of Isaac; and Jesus was affixed to a cross upon which He perished.

Not as much was written about Isaac compared to the other patriarchs. But enough was written for us to know that he worshipped G-d, and yet he had some shortcomings and was not without sin. He could not be the sacrifice for the sins of the world, but G-d had him go through this exercise to point the way to the one who could.

Joseph's Heart of Forgiveness: Joseph was his dad's favorite, which caused his brothers to be jealous. As time went on, his brothers reached a point where they could not stand the sight of him. They almost killed him, but instead they sold him into slavery in a foreign land. There he suffered for thirteen years. Rather than wallowing in bitterness and self-pity, Joseph turned to G-d. G-d was with him all those dark days. One day, Joseph's circumstances turned around. The narrative slows down at this point, as G-d wants us to pay attention to this part of Joseph's life. Genesis chapters 42 through 45 cover Joseph's forgiveness of his brothers and reconciliation with them. As we saw in our chapter on Joseph, his brothers encountered him many years after they sinned against him, when he was in a position of great power in Egypt. They did not recognize him, and he used his position to put them through a test. Joseph did not do this to exact a measure of justice, for he had already forgiven them in his heart. But rather, he did this because he wanted to be reconciled with his brothers. But reconciliation requires the willingness of both parties. Therefore, Joseph made this effort to try to save his relationship with them.

Similarly, Jesus was loathed by the religious leaders of the Jews. They were jealous of His popularity with the people, and they could not stand Him for the claims He made of being the Messiah and even of being G-d! They plotted against Him, and they succeeded. He was crucified on Passover in the early 30s CE. Jesus did not try to defend Himself against this ghastly sentence. He came for this purpose—to die for the sins of mankind. Joseph is a type of Jesus in that Joseph was tremendously forgiving of those who sinned against him and robbed him of the prime of his life. Furthermore, Joseph did not just want to relinquish them from having to pay a price for their sins and be done with them. Rather, he wanted to be restored to a healthy relationship with them. So too, Jesus gave up His life in order to provide forgiveness to sinners, including His enemies.[246] Ever since, He has been knocking on the doors of people's hearts and offering them salvation in an attempt to be reconciled with them. In the words of Jesus:

> "Behold, I stand at the door and knock; if anyone hears My voice and opens the door, I will come in to him, and will dine with him, and he with Me."[247]

Moses the Mediator: What an amazing life Moses led. He dealt with the wicked pharaoh, and he knew G-d intimately. Although Moses was not perfect, he was humble and he loved G-d and his fellow man deeply. It is no wonder that Moses was such a great leader of the nation. In Exodus chapters 32 through 34 is the story of Moses advocating on behalf of the Jews for their release from judgement for their thoughtless rebellion. As we saw earlier in our chapter on Moses, a couple of his statements really stand out:

> And the L-rd said to Moses, "I have seen this people, and behold, they are an obstinate people. Now then let Me alone, that My anger may burn against them, and that I may destroy them; and I will make of you a great nation."
>
> Then Moses entreated the L-rd his G-d, and said, "O L-rd, why doth Thine anger burn against Thy people whom Thou hast brought out from the land of Egypt with great power and with a mighty hand? Why should the

---

[246] Acts 2:22-23; 37-41.
[247] Rev. 3:20.

Egyptians speak, saying, 'With evil *intent* He brought them out to kill them in the mountains and to destroy them from the face of the earth'? Turn from Thy burning anger and change Thy mind about *doing* harm to Thy people. Remember Abraham, Isaac, and Israel, Thy servants to whom Thou didst swear by Thyself, and didst say to them, 'I will multiply your descendants, as the stars of the heavens, and all this land of which I have spoken I will give to your descendants, and they shall inherit *it* forever.'" So the L-rd changed His mind about the harm which He said He would do to His people.[248]

and,

And it came about on the next day that Moses said to the people, "You yourselves have committed a great sin; and now I am going up to the L-rd, perhaps I can make atonement for your sin." Then Moses returned to the L-rd, and said, "Alas, this people has committed a great sin, and they have made a god of gold for themselves. But now, if Thou wilt, forgive their sin—and if not, please blot me out from Thy book which Thou hast written!"[249]

In the first set of verses, G-d informed Moses of the Jews' rebellion; and Moses made a legal case for why the Jews'

---

[248] Ex. 32:9-14.
[249] Ex. 32:30-32.

sentence should be waived. Namely, it would be better for G-d not to wipe all the Jews out, except for Moses and his family, for the sake of His reputation amongst the Gentiles. In addition, Moses called on G-d to remember and honor the promises He made to Abraham, Isaac, and Jacob. G-d was pleased with Moses' arguments, and He rescinded His threat against the Jews.

As we saw earlier, following this interaction with G-d, Moses went down the mountain and saw for himself the spectacle of the Jews being "out of control" as they engaged in some form of sexual perversion in their worship of their new manmade god.[250] It was then that Moses fully grasped how guilty the Jews were. So, he went back up the mountain to plead with G-d again.

Moses' new argument is in the second set of verses above. Here, he simply confessed to G-d their great sin and asked for forgiveness. Moses also asked to be blotted out of G-d's book if G-d was not going to forgive the Jews. Moses was sincere. He had given his heart to leading this people and he loved them. G-d responded that there would be some level of punishment for the Jews, but nonetheless, they would go on and Moses would continue leading them.

Jesus is similar to Moses in that He is also a mediator between G-d and man. Furthermore, like Moses, Jesus' heart for sinners is unfathomable. But, whereas G-d did not blot Moses out of His book, He did pour out His wrath upon Jesus while Jesus was on the cross.[251] Jesus came to pay the price for the sins of man, and He accomplished it! Today, Jesus is in heaven where He advocates before G-d for the release of

---

[250] Ex. 32:6, 25.
[251] Isa. 53:10; Mt. 27:46.

sinners from judgement based on the atonement He provided.[252]

Moses also foreshadowed Jesus in terms of the mission Jesus will perform when He returns to earth at the end of time. Moses took on Pharaoh, and he led the Jews from slavery in Egypt to freedom in the promised land. So too will Jesus put down the Antichrist and set the Jews free from foreign aggression forever.[253] Further, He will regather the Jews from around the world and lead them to Israel where they will experience G-d's blessing.

David's Act of Unconditional Love: David was like Moses in many ways. He lived an extraordinary life. He loved G-d deeply, and he was a great king and leader of the Jewish people. Of course, there were some differences between these two as well.

It is notable that G-d had Samuel record the story of Mephibosheth. For, this story is not really needed to explain the progression of history at that time. Mephibosheth was one of the last remaining descendants of King Saul. He was also the son of David's best friend, Jonathan.[254] Mephibosheth had become crippled in an accident when he was five years old. It happened as his nurse fled with him, thinking his life was in danger when Saul and Jonathan died in battle. She knew David would become the king, and she feared Mephibosheth would likely be killed.[255] For, it was standard practice in the ancient world for a new king to kill all the living descendants of the former king in order to remove any potential rivals.

---

[252] Heb. 7:25-27.

[253] Rev. 19:11-21.

[254] In addition, Mephibosheth had a young son named Mica. Therefore, Mica was a great grandson to King Saul (2 Sam. 9:12).

[255] 2 Sam. 4:4.

But David was not just any king in the ancient world. David was a Jew, and he loved G-d. Therefore, one day some years later, David inquired as to whether there was anyone left who was a descendant of Saul. This was not an issue that he had been concerned about before then. When David inquired, it was not to take Mephibosheth's life and tie up a loose end. But rather, quite extraordinarily, it was to "show him kindness for Jonathan's sake."[256] Mephibosheth was hiding and living in fear, but David discovered his whereabouts and had him transported to Jerusalem. From that point on, David did not just set Mephibosheth's mind at ease by letting him know that his life was not in danger. No, David's actions were much richer than that. From that day forward, Mephibosheth lived in the palace and ate with David as if he was one of David's sons. This was not a publicity stunt or even simply a nice gesture. This was an act of love. The Hebrew word 'ḥesed', which is a special word describing the deep love and compassion that G-d has for people, is used multiple times in 2 Samuel chapter 9 to describe the love David extended to Mephibosheth. In fact, David had been blessed so deeply by G-d that his thoughts were not self-protective, but rather, he contemplated how he could be a blessing to others.

G-d included this incident so that we could understand Him and His love a little bit better. The way David treated Mephibosheth is how G-d deals with us. G-d created each of us, He knows us, and He is watching us. Whenever anyone turns to G-d and receives Jesus' offer of atonement, it gives G-d joy. Then, He comes into our lives and fills our hearts with love like He did with David. Further, when our lives are done, we will enter His presence and get to know Him on an even deeper level than Moses did. It is not because of us; it is because of His beautiful, deep love for us. Jesus taught this

---

[256] 2 Sam. 9:1.

message, and He demonstrated it as He treated all who came to Him with warmth and acceptance, even the foulest of sinners.

David also typified Jesus' second coming as David was a great general and King. So too, Jesus, who is the heir to the throne of David, will deliver the Jews from the armies of the Gentile world when He returns. Then He will rule the world and establish peace and justice.[257]

Daniel's Emergence from the Lions' Den: Daniel was a great man of G-d. Compared to the rest of us, he was relatively sinless. In addition, he was brave and he would not compromise his faith even if it meant placing himself in grave danger. Similar to Isaac, the way Daniel typified Jesus the most was in his execution. But whereas Isaac's execution was aborted at the last moment, Daniel's execution was carried out as he was thrown into a lions' den. However, G-d intervened and Daniel lived. Isaac's event foreshadowed Jesus' crucifixion, and Daniel's event foreshadowed His resurrection.

In Daniel chapter 6 we learn that this beautiful, godly man was loved and appreciated by the Persian king above him as well as all the people who were under his authority. But his peers, the satraps and commissioners, were jealous of Daniel because the king planned to elevate him above them. Of course, Daniel was not competing with them; he was just following G-d. They should have followed G-d and learned to love G-d and people from their hearts like Daniel did. Then they would have been loved too. But instead, they plotted against Daniel. Their plot worked, and the king was forced to have Daniel thrown into a lions' den. In the morning, the king went to the lions' den and called Daniel to see if G-d saved

---

[257] Isa. 9:6-7 (5-6).

him. Indeed, G-d did and Daniel emerged from the lions' den alive and unharmed.

In Jesus' case, the jealous religious leaders in Judea plotted against Him and forced the hand of the Roman procurator, Pontius Pilate, to have Him executed. Pontius Pilate did not want to execute Jesus, but circumstances prevented him from overriding the demands of the Jews. So, he had Jesus crucified. Unlike Daniel, Jesus did perish. But then things played out as if they were following a script based on Daniel chapter 6. First, Jesus was laid to rest in a tomb. Then a large stone was placed over the opening, and a Roman seal was affixed to the stone to ensure that no one would take Jesus' body. In addition, a Roman guard detail was stationed outside of the tomb,[258] for Jesus had predicted that He would rise from the grave after three days.[259] The religious leaders desperately wanted that statement to be proven false so that the Jews' fascination with Jesus would start to die down. Therefore, they urged Pilate to guard the tomb, which he did. But, G-d had other plans. When Jesus' followers went to the tomb a few days later, they found the stone rolled away and the body missing. Then they found Jesus, alive, resurrected; and the Christian movement took off like a rocket ship.

Cyrus the Deliverer: Cyrus is the only Gentile to be given the title 'messiah' in the Hebrew Bible. Furthermore, before Cyrus was born, Isaiah prophesied that he would deliver the Jews. Isaiah even prophesied his name. Right on cue, a couple hundred years later, Cyrus rose to power in Persia and took down the heathen Babylonian emperor and his empire. Then Cyrus did something that caught everyone off guard. He was the emperor of a world empire, but he was benevolent to

---

[258] Mt. 27:62-66.
[259] Mt. 12:38-41.

foreign peoples! He outlawed slavery, and he respected freedom of religion. In addition, when Cyrus was shown the prophecy about him in the Hebrew Bible, he believed in the G-d of Israel and he bowed to Him.[260] The prophecy about Cyrus predicted that he would shepherd the Jews back to Judah to rebuild Jerusalem and the Temple. And so he did.[261] Thus, Cyrus is a type of Jesus' second coming. For Jesus will come back and put down the future evil world emperor and his empire. In fact, He will end the oppressive self-governance of the Gentile world forever at that point. Then He will regather all of the Jews to their homeland and rule the world from Jerusalem. Needless to say, He will rule benevolently and for the good of all mankind.

Jesus' First Coming: Joseph's choice to forgive his brothers and his fight to be reconciled with them; Moses' heart for the Jewish people, his willingness to be judged alongside them, and his advocacy on their behalf; David's act of lavishing kindness, gifts, and acceptance on Mephibosheth; Isaac's trial run of dying as a sacrifice; and Daniel's emergence alive from confinement with a pack of lions all forecast the key elements of Jesus' mission two thousand years ago. In Jesus' words, He "did not come to be served, but to serve, and to give His life a ransom for many."[262] Paul explained Jesus' role in G-d's plan as follows:

> Blessed *be* the G-d and Father of our L-rd Jesus Christ, who has blessed us with every spiritual blessing in the heavenly *places* in Christ, just as He chose us in Him before the

---

[260] Isa. 44:26b-45:6.

[261] 2 Chron. 36:23.

[262] Mt. 20:28.

foundation of the world, that we should be holy and blameless before Him. In love He predestined us to adoption as sons through Jesus Christ to Himself, according to the kind intention of His will, to the praise of the glory of His grace, which He freely bestowed on us in the Beloved. In Him we have redemption through His blood, the forgiveness of our trespasses, according to the riches of His grace, which He lavished upon us.[263]

The moment Adam and Eve rebelled, G-d set in motion a plan to provide forgiveness and offer reconciliation to people. But, it required Jesus to come and pay the price of justice on our behalf. Those who say yes to Jesus' kind offer will become "holy and blameless." The thing that no High Priest was ever able to do, to fully enter G-d's presence, those who receive Jesus will freely do! For they will always be welcome in His presence as His adopted, beloved children.

This sounds too good to be true. So, even the drug pusher who sells fentanyl to teens in pursuit of filthy money can go to heaven simply by saying 'yes' to Jesus? The answer is yes. How can this be? The reason is because we are not dealing with another morally compromised human, we are dealing with G-d, who is rich in ḥesed. We are Mephibosheth. He was severely handicapped, and we are morally handicapped. Mephibosheth called himself a "dead dog," and so he would have been as a descendant of the former king in any other land on earth. But the new king was David. David had a relationship with G-d and he knew G-d's love. Furthermore, David had made a covenant with Mephibosheth's father. So instead of being put to death, Mephibosheth was welcomed

---

[263] Eph. 1:3-8a.

into David's presence as a son! So too, G-d made a unilateral covenant with Abraham. This covenant was for Abraham's descendants, the Jews, but it also included "all the families of the earth." We can count on G-d to honor the covenant He made. This is why Jesus came, and this is how we can go to heaven and be welcomed into G-d's presence. So, yes, even the drug pusher, even the pedophile, even me with my filthy sins, and even you can go to heaven.

In addition to the acts of Isaac, Joseph, Moses, David, and Daniel foreshadowing the heart of Jesus' mission, there are also ancillary details from their lives that are similar to things that happened to Jesus. For example, both Joseph and Jesus were unceremoniously disrobed by their attackers. Joseph's brothers took the special coat Jacob gave him and soaked it in blood to deceive their father into thinking that Joseph had been eaten by a wild animal.[264] In Jesus' case, the Roman soldiers famously gambled for His tunic which was seamless.[265] These parallel details serve to get our attention and help us to see the connections between each of these men and Jesus.

Jesus' Second Coming: Jesus said that He would return.[266] And so He will. When He comes back, it will be to liberate the Jewish people as Moses did. First, He will smash the Gentile armies. It will be along the lines of the Egyptian soldiers drowning in the Red Sea or the 185,000 Assyrian soldiers perishing in their camp at night during the reign of King Hezekiah.[267] Only, this time, hundreds of millions of soldiers

---

[264] Gen. 37:31-35.
[265] Jn. 19:23-24.
[266] Mt. 24:3, 24-39; Acts 1:9-11.
[267] Isa. 37:36.

will die, not hundreds of thousands. In Psalm 2, there is a question:

> Why are the nations in an uproar, and the peoples devising a vain thing? The kings of the earth take their stand, and the rulers take counsel together against the L-rd and against His Anointed: "Let us tear their fetters apart, and cast away their cords from us!"[268]

This prophetic psalm about the end of time was written by David. In it he asks why the nations would ever attempt such a vain and futile thing—to defy the one true G-d, the all-powerful creator of heaven and earth. Of course, we tried this before, at the dawn of history. Namely, in Genesis chapter 11, the people united to build a great city with a tall tower in order to show G-d their capability and notify Him that they were breaking free from His authority. G-d observed the city and its tower, and He also observed their sinful hearts. Then He took action and separated them and gave them different languages. He did this for their sakes, for sin begets more sin and the result is destruction. To think that man would make the same mistake in the twenty-first century is hard to fathom. Certainly, we have increased our understanding of science and the arts, but apparently, we have not grown any wiser. We still think G-d and Jesus are our problems, and we still think that we can overthrow them. Once again, G-d will step in and put down the rebellion. This time it will be Jesus who will put an end to this ludicrous military attempt to rebel against G-d.

Needless to say, just like Cyrus' victory over the Babylonians, so too will Jesus' victory be lightening quick. In the blink of an eye, Jesus will end the reign of the future world

---

[268] Ps. 2:1-3.

emperor, the Antichrist. For, just like King Belshazzar all those years ago, the Antichrist will brazenly oppose G-d and be found wanting.

Following the end of Gentile rule, Jesus will guide the Jews who are scattered around the world back to their land. Only, this time, as opposed to Moses' leading of the Jews through the desert, the journey will be much smoother. In fact, just as Moses spoke to G-d during the first journey, so too, all the Jews will speak with Jesus. They will each get to know Him, and it will change them. Here is what will happen as they make their way to Israel.

> Like a shepherd He will tend His flock, in His arm He will gather the lambs, and carry *them* in His bosom; He will gently lead the nursing *ewes*.[269]

and,

> . . . the ransomed of the L-rd will return, and come with joyful shouting to Zion, with everlasting joy upon their heads. They will find gladness and joy, and sorrow and sighing will flee away.[270]

A lot of lies have been told about G-d. Most of the people of the world will believe these lies at the end of time. But the truth is that G-d is loving beyond our ability to comprehend. These Jews will experience G-d's love on their journey home.

---

[269] Isa. 40:11.
[270] Isa. 35:10.

Never again will the Jews have to flee. This time sorrow and suffering will flee! The word 'joy' is used three times in the bottom verse. The Jews will experience a deep, healing joy on the day of their regathering.

Following the regathering, Jesus will rule the world while sitting on the throne of his forefather, David. David was a great king, but he was human. He led the people to worship and obey G-d. Yet, he also succumbed to temptation and caused a great deal of damage in his family and in Israel. But Jesus is G-d, and He will be righteous.

TO BE CONTINUED. . .

INDEX

Ḥesed is available at a discounted price as an e-book. It is available at the regular price as a paperback or an audiobook.

All profits will be donated to
Yad Vashem—
The World Holocaust Remembrance Center.
Please visit lovingkindnessofadonai.com for updates on the amount donated to Yad Vashem.

Volume Two: *The Māshîaḥ* is also available.